Wind bands and brass bands in school and music centre

KEVIN THOMPSON

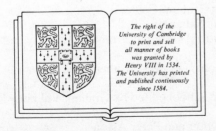

The right of the
University of Cambridge
to print and sell
all manner of books
was granted by
Henry VIII in 1534.
The University has printed
and published continuously
since 1584.

CAMBRIDGE UNIVERSITY PRESS

Cambridge
London   New York   New Rochelle
Melbourne   Sydney

≡RESOURCES OF MUSIC≡

General Editor: John Paynter

Books for the Classroom

Cantors by Mary Berry
Minstrels 2 by Brian Sargent
Poverty Knock by Roy Palmer
Something to Play by Geoffrey Brace
Strike the Bell by Roy Palmer
The Painful Plough by Roy Palmer
The Rigs of the Fair by Roy Palmer and Jon Raven
The Valiant Sailor by Roy Palmer
Troubadours by Brian Sargent
Troubadours and Minstrels, record (Brian Sargent)

Books for Teachers

Electronic Music for Schools by Richard Orton
Folk Music in School edited by Robert Leach and Roy Palmer
Jazz by Graham Collier
Jazz: Illustrations, record (Graham Collier)
Jazz: Lecture Concert, record (Graham Collier)
Living School Music by William Salaman
Pop Music in School (New Edition) edited by Graham Vulliamy and
    Ed Lee
Pop Music in School: Illustrations, cassette (Graham Vulliamy and
    Ed Lee)
Pop, Rock and Ethnic Music in School edited by Graham Vulliamy and
    Ed Lee
Sound and Silence by John Paynter and Peter Aston
Sound and Silence, record (John Paynter and Peter Aston)
Vibrations by David Sawyer

Contents

To *BASBWE*, *NSBA* and *WASBE*

Published by the Press Syndicate of the University of Cambridge
The Pitt Building, Trumpington Street, Cambridge CB2 1RP
32 East 57th Street, New York, NY 10022, USA
10 Stamford Road, Oakleigh, Melbourne 3166, Australia

First published 1985

Printed in Great Britain at the University Press, Cambridge

Library of Congress catalogue card number: 84 – 12118

British Library cataloguing in publication data
Thompson, Kevin
Wind bands and brass bands in school and
music centre. – (Resources of music)
1. School music – Instruction and study –
Great Britain   2. Brass bands – Instruction
and study – Great Britain   3. Wind instruments
– Instruction and study – Great Britain
I. Title   II. Series
785′.06′71   MT3.G7
ISBN 0 521 25892 8 hard covers
ISBN 0 521 27750 7 paperback

Diagrams by Len Huxter

WD

Foreword

When I was young in the early years of this century a rollicking popular ditty contained the lines:

I do like to stroll along the Prom, Prom, Prom,
Where the brass bands play Tiddely-om-pom-pom!

This aptly expressed the average person's reaction to band music at that time.

Later on, in the early twenties, I found myself involved to some extent in military and brass band music and I had somehow to learn about the constitution of these bodies and how to write for them. It was not possible to get full scores of military band music as publishers only issued 'short scores' on two, or sometimes three staves with some indication of instrumentation.

Brass band scores were, however, available. Apart from marches, the repertoires of both media consisted of arrangements only. Selections from Gilbert and Sullivan were staple fare, as were selections from the latest musical comedies and revues, and from forgotten operas and operettas of Victorian times, not to mention waltzes by Johann Strauss and Waldteufel. I was rewarded by discovering a brass band score entitled *Ten Minutes with Richard Wagner*.

Kevin Thompson's unique book reminds us of how much things in the worlds of wind and brass bands have changed. There is now a very large library of works specifically composed for one or other of these media and scoring for them has become as imaginative and resourceful as is orchestration – in fact wind bands are often called wind orchestras.

In order to become a good wind instrument player it is necessary to start young, and this book is mainly concerned with the training of those of school age. Quite young girls can learn to play even the largest instruments, such as euphoniums and tubas, and thoroughly enjoy it.

Though primarily designed to help and inspire school teachers and those who coach and conduct at music centres, the book deals with technical problems encountered by the players and by those who write and score for bands.

v

Dr Thompson's ideas on scoring are not only applicable to writing for inexperienced school bands but are generally to be recommended for bands of all stages and proficiency.

For instance, he believes in giving players plenty of rests and using the band in sections instead of trying to find something for everyone to do all the time, and he is equally in favour of clarity, transparency and contrast in writing for the more homogeneous brass band medium.

All this makes the full band more thrilling when it is used and makes everything more interesting for the listeners, and more comfortable for the players, who soon get tired if worked too hard.

This book is certainly what it professes to be – a practical manual. But it is written by one who is not only experienced in every branch of his special subject but is a dedicated and sensitive musician as well.

I feel sure that this book will be warmly welcomed by all those who are in any way concerned with wind and brass bands. Conductors, players, composers and arrangers will all find valuable help and stimulus from the sound sense and wisdom in its pages.

Gordon Jacob 1984

Sadly, Gordon Jacob died while this book was in preparation.

Preface

The following is intended as a handbook for all those concerned with wind bands and brass bands in schools and music centres. As with any handbook it is essentially pragmatic and the main body of the text is concerned with method, material and organisation, prefaced and placed in perspective by historical and present-day issues.

The text falls into four parts: the first two the reader will find of a general nature, applicable to both types of bands, the second two more specific. From a brief account of times past – retracing the development of the band – we turn to times present, document recent developments, and clarify the current scene. Our next concern is to formulate a rationale for including wind bands and brass bands in school and music centre. We then take a wider view, indicating the place of instrumental music within the curriculum and drawing together classroom and group instrumental lessons.

From there the text divides into two further parts: one dealing with wind bands; the other with brass bands. In each, the practical difficulties of putting together the embryonic band are discussed, along with rehearsal points and scoring schemes to suit the most likely combinations.

As concern for material is central to the premise, each section is rounded off with repertoire suggestions.

We have in the space of the last few years seen a tremendous growth in the numbers of educationally-based bands. Such interest, however, cannot be localised to Britain. Some countries sniffed the wind of change long ago. Whilst in Britain there has been an upsurge of wind bands, America has enjoyed a rebirth of the British-style brass band. Indeed, the band movement as a whole is now a truly international affair.

Although evolved from the same genesis, wind bands and brass bands have led entirely separate lives and bred two quite separate natures. The American model shows what might have been had we kept with the woodwind: the British model shows what might have been had the Americans retained an all-brass combination. But, as history relates, this was not to be the case. Only now are we beginning to share each other's enthusiasms and benefit from each other's expertise.

It is interesting too to compare the music and literature of the two types of band. Whereas the first real works for wind band were written in the 1790s (those composed for the celebrated band of the Garde Nationale by Gossec, Catel, Jadin and Méhul) the repertoire for brass band is very much a twentieth-century story. And whilst on the brass band there are several references, for the wind band – as distinct from the military band – there is not a single British book. It is hoped that the present text will contribute in some measure towards resolving this situation, as well as fill some of the lacunae encountered as soon as we venture outside our own specialism. It makes, I hope, for a pertinent and rich source book.

Kevin Thompson 1984

Acknowledgements

I am indebted to the following persons: Professor Keith Swanwick, for his guidance with the group instrumental chapter; Dorothy Taylor, for reading the first draft of historical and present-day perspectives; the late John Moutrie for his assistance with the class band chapters; Professor John Paynter for his editorial emendations; Rosemary Davidson (CUP), who foresaw the possibilities of the book; W.G. and B. Devonald for their help with preparation of the manuscript for publication, and the late Dr Gordon Jacob CBE, who not only acceded to my request that he pen a foreword, but with characteristic humility responded as if the honour were his.

Thanks are due also to Wallace Berry, National Wind Band of Scotland; Geoffrey Brand; Arthur Butterworth; Edward Buttress, *British Mouthpiece*; Bradley Catto, National Youth Brass Band of Scotland; Ian Christie, North West Wind Society; Derek Farnell, Military and Concert Band Association; Edward Gregson; Roy Newsome; Timothy Reynish; Philip Sparke; Denzil Stephens, *Brass Band News*; Charles Sweby MBE, National School Band Association; Peter Wilson, *British Bandsman*; Roger Wright, British Music Information Centre; and others too numerous to mention, who in discussion or by correspondence have given so freely of their advice.

In closing, to my wife Patricia, herself a busy musician, I extend a special note of gratitude for her indispensable assistance throughout each stage of the book's production. A hard time she had of it.

Acknowledgement must be made of the following publishers for permission to quote extracts from their copyright material: Belwin Mills for 'Band Today' by James Ployhar; Chappell for *Psalm 104* by Anthony Hedges, and 'Song from MASH' by Johnny Mandel; Hal Leonard for 'Scarborough Fair'; Joad Press for *A Traditional Hornpipe Suite* by Adrian Cruft; Merion Music for *Stone Images* by Sidney Hodkinson; Northern Songs for 'Here, There and Everywhere', and 'Yesterday' by John Lennon and Paul McCartney; Novello for *Sinfonietta* by Joseph Horovitz; Oxford University Press for *Flourish for Wind Band* by Vaughan Williams, *First Tunes and Studies for the Trombone or*

x   **Acknowledgements**

Euphonium by Bram Wiggins, and *Vivat Regina* by William Mathias; R. Smith for *Saturday Market* by Anthony Hedges, *Intrada* by Pezel, *Marche de la Procession Dansante* and *Proclamation and Folk Song* by Kevin Thompson; Standard Music for 'Sing' by Joe Raposo; Patersons Publications Ltd for *Little Suite for Brass* by Malcolm Arnold; James Tenney for *Swell Piece* from *Postal Pieces* 1954–71; Weinberger for *Count Down* by Paul Patterson.

The Publishers have been unable to trace the copyright holder for 'Without You' by Peter Ham and Tom Evans. However, they will be happy to come to a suitable arrangement at the earliest opportunity.

Part I ORIGINS AND RATIONALE

1 Historical and present-day perspectives

The band has a long tradition. Its roots can be found in three main sources: in town waits, in royal and ceremonious music,and in the military bands of medieval times. Town waits continued until 1835 when they were abolished by legislation which paradoxically benefited the movement since it prompted players to instigate their own bands. Music and religion have always been interrelated but it was not until the sixteenth century that bands were employed to accompany church services.

In the eighteenth century there were two major influences: firstly, the exotic Turkish military bands from which many of the modern percussion instruments have developed; and secondly, the '*harmonie*', the court wind band of the eighteenth-century European aristocracy – a band comprising two oboes, two clarinets, two bassoons and two horns. The prime function of the *harmonie* was to provide background music for court soirées, hence the distinct absence of the heavier brass and percussion instruments. It was for this ensemble that Mozart wrote his E flat Serenade K375, considered a classic of the genre.

When, in the aftermath of the French revolution, the fashionable Paris Opera closed (a venue once frequented by the aristocracy), the musicians of the opera orchestra simply enlisted into the ranks of the newly-formed wind bands of the republic. Foremost amongst these bands was the revolutionary Garde Nationale, a band of forty-five players whose influence was to be far-reaching. From this group, established in Paris in 1789 with Captain Sarette as its bandmaster, many of the European and American wind bands developed. Sarette founded the Paris Conservatoire largely to foster wind bands, and many of his colleagues from the Garde Nationale were appointed to its staff.

Coincidentally, country bands – popular imitations of the court bands but consisting of almost any wind instrument to hand – became a focal point of village life. It is from these that many of today's renowned brass bands stem. Besses o' th' Barn, named after the inn in which the band rehearsed, is perhaps the best-known example, although the band did not change its title until it became all-brass in 1853 and was formerly known as Clegg's Reed Band. Clegg's, because it was financed and staffed (though naturally not entirely) by the Clegg brothers, Joseph, James and John. Reed, as this was a term used to denote woodwind and brass, its instrumentation comprising: F clarionet; three C clarionets; piccolo; keyed bugle; trumpet; French horn; trombone; bass horn; and bass drum. Similarly, Brighouse and Rastrick began as a brass and reed band, as did Black Dyke Mills which first appeared in 1816 as Peter Wharton's Brass and Reed Band.

Wind band competitions on any organised scale began in 1845 at the Hall of Burton Constable, the home of Sir Clifford Constable – not, it might be thought, fertile ground for the seeding of brass band contests. But, however insignificant it seemed at the time, it was to set a precedent. Within a few years regular contesting was initiated in nearby Hull and other Northern venues. This led to the famous Belle Vue and Crystal Palace brass band contests, thanks largely to the endeavours of one Enderby Jackson who had been an impressionable eighteen-year-old flautist with a competing band at Burton Constable. It was he also who was to manage the European tour of the American Gilmore Band in 1878.

Innovations in the design of brass instruments, in particular the invention of the piston valve (brought about largely by Adolphe Sax, although controversy still remains over the originality of some of his work) led to an all-brass combination which eventually gave rise to brass bands and caused the subsequent demise of the civilian wind band in this country. Initially, many of the newly-improved brass instruments were purchased by wealthy industrial benefactors for their work force to play in their all-too-short evenings after work.

To this day brass bands find themselves defending paternalism in the form of sponsorship, although nowadays many of the players are not sponsored by their own employers. In the space of the last few years, sponsorship (in the form of large sums of money for matching sets of high quality instruments) has become inseparable from the sounds of many of our top bands. Whilst he who pays the piper may not yet be in a position to call the tune (nor should such a position be allowed to eventuate) he may certainly help the tune to ring true. The wonder is not that subsidy from commerce and business should return, but that many bands have continued for so long without it. For all the resurgence of interest in sponsorship, the brass band remains essentially an amateur phenomenon. Of the sponsored bands, the name of John Foster, associated with the same band since 1855, is billed above the title in the implied possessive case, John Foster & Son Ltd, Black Dyke Mills Band; of the independent bands, Brighouse and Rastrick, whose royalties from record sales of *The Floral Dance* enabled the band to build its own concert hall, is undoubtedly the most renowned.

Whilst a few of the bandsmen of today are, in effect, semi-professionals, the majority, if they do not actually pay for the privilege of playing (and most of them do), meet the cost of small expenses from out of their own pockets. Low cost brass band music then, has become a necessity.

Richard Smith, evidently a remarkable cornettist and a widely respected teacher, founded the *Champion Brass Band Journal* in Hull in 1859. Taking on the rôles of editor and publisher, R. Smith (to become the name of the publishing company), issued inexpensive scores and parts for brass bands. It was his firm that later, under the proprietorship of John Henry Iles, was to lay claim to many of the classics of the repertoire.

The entrepreneurial John Henry Iles devoted much of his life to brass band music and brought a new zest to the medium. He took over the ownership of *The British Bandsman* from Samuel Cope, whom he retained as editor, and in 1900 organised an immense concert bringing together eleven bands in the Royal Albert Hall including Besses o' th' Barn and Black Dyke Mills. There was, seemingly, a capacity audience of two thousand and the proceeds from the concert went to aid dependants of those fighting in the Boer war. A chance remark by Sir Arthur Sullivan, the conductor of the concert and a director of the Crystal Palace, gave Iles – who recalled the contests Enderby Jackson had organised in the 1860s – the idea of holding an annual contest there and almost an automatic entrée. And so the National Championships (at which in later years John Henry Iles could be seen *en grande tenue*, wearing his OBE), came into being and brass banding had, as it were, come of age. But the developing years of the movement were earlier and three legendary rivals dominated them.

Such characters as Gladney, Swift and Owen, could hardly be fabricated. To the bandsmen whom they led time and again to the victory dais they were heroes indeed. John Gladney has been called the father of the movement. With his highly successful Meltham Mills Band, he did much to standardise the instrumentation since other bands adopted its prize-winning line-up. Edwin Swift, a self-taught musician, did not relinquish his job as a handloom weaver until his thirty-second birthday. As if the late start were an obligation to work diligently, he continued to improve himself all the time and was in great demand conducting Linthwaite and a dozen or so other bands. The third member of this triumvirate of itinerant professional band trainers was Alexander Owen, who was, it appears, something of a martinet. Nowadays he is best remembered for his stunning arrangements, for bringing Black Dyke Mills Band to the fore, and for his triumphant, eighteen-month world tour with Besses o' th' Barn – the idea of the tour was conceived by none other than John Henry Iles.

In the wake of these early pioneers, Gladney, Swift and Owen, there followed a veritable succession of highly accomplished band trainers: Rimmer; Halliwell; Greenwood; Mortimers, father and sons. Such men were not only to mould and shape the sound of the British brass band, but by their band's performances, were to define it in a class of its own.

On the continent the brass and reed bands became known, confusingly, as '*harmonie*', although nowadays these are larger than the old court bands of the same name. In addition to this, in France there is the '*fanfare*' as distinct from the '*harmonie*', a predominantly although not entirely brass ensemble; and in Germany, the '*posaunchöre*', a kind of all-brass equivalent of the early church bands.

Back in Britain, whilst the brass band came into being largely through the philanthropic attitude and desire of mill millionaires and cotton kings that their workers should spend their scant leisure time in worthwhile pursuits, the development of the wind band was left almost entirely to the military. Kneller Hall, converted into a school of music, began classes in 1857.

Bashford (*Music Teacher*, 59, 8 (1980) p. 9) estimates that over a thousand bandmasters and over a quarter of a million bandsmen have passed through the school since it began. Further to this, many of these bandsmen contributed to the growth of wind bands in schools:

> Retired army bandmasters found a new release for their expertise, at first in many of the Public Schools and later more widely. The results of a number of these 'instructors', as they were frequently termed, were to be seen in the formation of wind ensembles for all ages . . . (*Music Teacher*, 57, 10 (1978) pp. 13–14).

But, in deference to military bands, it is to America that we have to turn for the development of wind bands as we have come to know them today (although many of the early bands were of a quasi-military type – a tradition upheld by the American marching bands). The reasons for the American predilection for wind bands are unclear, but there appear to be several contributory factors. Emigrés, in particular Moravians, imported European *harmoniemusik* into America where it remained in vogue into the nineteenth century.

In England, anything to do with music used to have class connotations and still does to some extent. The social structure of America was more egalitarian, and therefore more able to accept wind bands into its culture, than Victorian England where the penchant of the middle-classes was for drawing-room and ballroom music. In sharp contrast, the

5   Historical and present-day perspectives

brass band in Britain was an 'exclusively' working-class phenomenon, and as Brand points out in *Brass Bands in the 20th Century* (Egon Publishers, 1979) 'the cloth cap image hung over brass bands for well over one hundred years.'

The legendary American pioneer-conductors Conway, Gilmore, Goldman, Pryor and undoubtedly the best-known, Sousa, had an unprecedented influence on the great American band. From the late sixties to the closing years of the nineteenth century the American fondness for spectacle was aptly demonstrated in epic, large-scale concerts involving massed bands and huge choruses of school children. Two gigantic festivals, the National Peace Jubilee in 1869 and the World Peace Jubilee of 1871, brought Gilmore international recognition which in turn Sousa and Pryor were to gain. Sousa's band, reputed for its all-American patriotic sound, so characteristic of the 1890s, did much to raise the standards of playing by extensively touring both internationally and at home. Later, Pryor, formerly Sousa's principal trombonist, organised his own band which was to become renowned worldwide for over thirty years.

Just as in Britain wealthy industrialists had financed instrumental purchases, many of the American high school and collegiate bands came into being as a result of business and civic backing. It is interesting to compare the transatlantic attitude of college and university bands with our own; only recently have three British conservatoires opened their doors to brass band instrumentalists, a fact that poses the question of class divisions today.

Throughout America, woodwind sections were enlarged to balance the brass. There began to be an emphasis on concert hall rather than alfresco performances, and an aesthetic re-evaluation of the band as a performing medium took place, due in no small part to the efforts of Frederick Fennell and the Eastman Wind Ensemble (see a review by R. Garofalo (1980) of Ostling, A.E., unpublished Ph.D thesis).

In the 1950s, Fennell strove to emulate the timbre of the brass and wind sections of the orchestra, performed original brass and wind music of all periods, and advocated the use of one player per part in a reaction to oversized bands. Today the American band movement is a multi-million dollar industry. There are many noted ensembles: the American Wind Symphony, the Cleveland Symphonic Winds, the Eastman Wind Ensemble, Ithaca High School Band, Michigan State University Wind Symphony – the list could go on and on. Illustrious conductors such as Battisti, Everett, Fennell, Hunsberger, Johnson, Paynter, Revelli, Reynolds, Whitwell, and more can be found working throughout the United States, and there is similar activity in Austria, Canada, France, Holland, Japan, Norway, Sweden and Switzerland. Latterly, Australia, a traditional bastion of the brass band movement, is reportedly turning to wind bands.

We might wonder why until recently wind band and brass band players have been slow to explore each other's medium – to cross the wind/all-brass divide. Of course some players (the lower brass) are to this day separated by clef but at one time the bands themselves were mutually exclusive in terms of each other's pitch. British military (wind) bands converted to universal pitch during the 1920s (hardly before time) but not until the 1960s, when manufacturers refused to continue producing high pitch instruments, did brass bands follow suit, so this discrepancy existed for almost forty years. It is far from surprising then that being cut off not merely from wind bands, but more importantly from the entire musical mainland during the long period when high pitch predominated, reinforced the cultural isolation of brass bands and made even top echelon players (whose technique is simply staggering) ineffectual musical travellers.

It would be out of place to argue the pros and cons of either brass bands or wind bands. Comparison is unfair and is analogous to comparing different kinds of orchestral combinations. Obviously there are palpable differences in style between wind bands and brass bands (instrumentation apart) but they share several important traits. It seems to be a fundamental misconception that the two are diametrically opposed; it is much more profitable to consider what one can give to the other. There is room for both to co-exist and the advantages that might accrue from interaction would be mutual.

1952 saw the founding of two organisations which were to have an unprecedented effect upon the development of the brass band in schools: the formation of the National Schools Brass Band Association and the National Youth Brass Band of Great Britain.

The decision to form an organisation which would foster the development of brass bands in schools was made by Lance Caisley and Kenneth Cook in as unlikely a setting as Christchurch harbour during the summer of 1952. The organisation came to be known as the NSBBA, and within six months of its inception it had a membership of some twenty bands as well as a number of supporting individuals. Determined to build on their auspicious beginning, Messrs Caisley and Cook set about organising a conference to which many eminent musicians of the day were invited, several of whom were to become members of a panel of advisers, the Association's Advisory Council.

Amongst the panel members was the publisher Max Hinrichsen who, through his publishing house, was to play a pivotal rôle in fulfilling the Association's aim of making music available which would be suitable for school bands. That this was one of the pressing needs of the day there is little doubt, for there was a dearth of adaptable brass band music from which to teach the young initiates coming forward. Yet the Association's advocacy was not simply to make suitable music available but to provide music of quality. Hinrichsen in conjunction with the Association, undertook to publish quality music to meet the requirements of school bands, even though with such a small nucleus of NSBBA members, the return on his initial investment could be nothing less than long term.

In addition to the eventual publication of the *First Band Book*, and the *Brass Band Journal*, an important landmark was reached with the publication in 1954 of *Music Through the Brass Band*, a handbook co-written by the founders of the NSBBA, with a foreword by Eric Ball. Within the same year the Association's first of many festivals took place. Non-competitive festivals at which individual bands play to one another and mass under the direction of a distinguished guest conductor have, together with courses for non-specialist teachers, become an integral part of the Association's work.

The inaugural course of the National Youth Brass Band took place in Bradford at Easter 1952, which antedated the formation of the NSBBA by several months. The counterpart of the National Youth Orchestra, the NYBB was founded by Denis Wright, who could have justly piqued himself on his substantial achievement. It was he who became its Music Adviser, a position he was to retain until 1967 when Geoffrey Brand took over the mantle.

What part the band has played, through its twice-yearly residential courses, in the development and encouragement of young brass band players generally can only be conjectured, though it is reassuring that not a few of the renowned orchestral brass players of today have at one stage been amongst its number. But whatever effect the band has had within the movement since its inception, the extent to which its influence has permeated outside (other than through its players graduating into the orchestral world at large) has been negligible. Indeed it is fair to say that it has never been considered with the same high regard as its orchestral equivalent, though that in no way diminishes Denis Wright's achievement in realising a national brass band of fine young players.

Although a few works have been especially written for the band, until now the commissioning of new music, augmenting the existing repertoire, has not been a prime concern. However, the Scots order things differently. It was not until 1958 – some six years after the founding of the NYBB – that, at the instigation of the Scottish Amateur Music Association, the initiative to form a National Youth Brass Band of Scotland was taken. The wonder is that the NYBBS is not older. Drake Rimmer became the band's first director and the tutorial staff were drawn from Kneller Hall. Since those early years, Denis Wright, Cedric Thorpe Davie, Bryden Thomson and Geoffrey Brand have in turn been its conductors – Thomson and Brand being the band's only permanent ones.

The band's celebrated record of commissioned works is not merely a part of the annals of the band itself, but can almost be taken as a short history of the development of twentieth-century brass band literature over the last twenty years. Several of the works listed lie at the heart of the contemporary repertoire: their resonances have been deep and far-reaching. Without the Scottish Amateur Music Association which is responsible for the NYBBS commissions (the same body is responsible for those of the National Wind Band of Scotland), the repertoire would be devoid of Martin Dalby's *Music for a Brass Band* and Thea Musgrave's *Variations for Brass Band* – to mention but two distinguished scores.

Apart from the differences in commissioning policy between the two national bands, there are differences of policy in regard to repertoire. In particular, whereas the NYBB has taken a more yielding view of arrangements and transcriptions, its Scottish counterpart has determined to play only that originally conceived as brass band music.

Presently, greater opportunity exists for young instrumentalists leaving school to continue their music-making in amateur brass bands than in comparable wind bands. This is due not so much to a consciously-sought closer liaison between school and amateur brass bands, but more to the fact that there are comparatively fewer amateur wind bands to join.

Time was, during the sixties and seventies, when bandsmen felt that the surge of school instrumental activity would provide a ready, untapped source of eager young recruits. But if the artesian well ever existed, then there seemed little sign of its supply permeating through in any great quantity to amateur bands. And yet today the brass band movement, even without an influx of players trained in school bands, remains a substantial amateur pastime.

Whilst brass bands may have failed to encourage large numbers of school leavers to join them – though there are instances to conflict with this, of course – many provide group tuition for learners or have their own 'feeder' bands to ensure a constant supply of new players. They have, in effect, had to nourish their own roots. But for the moment we might turn our attention to the school leavers who have been integrated into brass bands. In their wake came new attitudes to the brass band. It gained a new-found acceptability, not least from the parents of those who had been taught through school lessons. If, in an attempt to participate in the social atmosphere of the brass band, there have been moments of class-conscious by-play between stalwarts and first generation players, it has largely gone unnoticed. Should, in the future, an influx of school-trained players in amateur brass bands eventuate – and one way in which links might be forged is by occasional shared concerts or workshops so that there exists a ready progression from school to community – then it is a nice point as to whether the new players will influence the bands, or the bands the players. On that we shall have to wait and see. One thing is certain, bands will have to range more widely over the substantial body of repertoire available to them rather than confining so much of their attention to dispensing a succession of largely, though not wholly, *passé* contest pieces for which there is often more cause for admiration of the technical demands made of the players, than occasion for musical stimulation. Without such stimulation, bands may find their new, more progressive members – perhaps to whom contesting is alien – wish to extricate themselves as quickly as possible. As our bands change, so must our music.

The relatively recent upsurge of interest in wind and brass instruments in schools is due, in part, to changes in the nature of society in the sixties. Trodd (*Music Teacher*, 57, 10 (1978), 13–14) looking retrospectively, cites three main causes for the phenomenon: firstly, children became avid listeners and, for the first time, avid purchasers of records; secondly, television was bringing them into closer contact with what had hitherto been only an aural experience; and thirdly, the emancipation of teenagers which led to a change of direction in music education.

Lawton (in *Handbook for Music Teachers*, Novello, 1968), writing in the sixties on the 'wind of change', emphasised that far from being unique to this country, the explosion of interest in wind and brass was part of a global trend. The reasons he cited were four-fold: the individualistic tone-colour of the majority of wind instruments and their sonority *en masse*; the greater use of wind by every modern composer from Berlioz and Wagner onwards; strong associations that wind is more up-to-date (*sic*); and finally the influence of the recorder. He drew attention to the Associated Board examination figures between the years 1961 to 1965 which show a doubling in the number of wind examinees of which fifty per cent were clarinettists, and to the proportionate balance in wind music sales of that time. Five years later the total number of wind and brass examinees had more than trebled from that of 1965 and again almost quadrupled the 1970 figure in 1979. Of course, on no account could it be said to be indicative of the actual number of wind and brass players in this country today. We can only speculate that the number is far in excess of that of the examinees and make conjectures on the basis of wind instrument sales and the volume of music crossing the Atlantic. Instrument manufacturers are markedly reluctant to divulge the extent of their sales.

One theory put forward suggests that certain personalities have given an extra boost to the popularity of these instruments. Undoubtedly, Atarah Ben Tovim, with her children's concerts led by Atarah's Band, has been important and James Galway, according to one retailer, has done more for flute sales than anyone. In the field of ensembles, Alan Hacker, with his Whispering Wind Band is redressing the balance from the trend for oversized ensembles, rather like a latter-day Frederick Fennell. Within the same circles, the London Saxophone Quartet, and the Double Reed Ensemble led by Dominic Muldowney are doing much to widen the scope of wind playing generally although it is doubtful that they exert much influence at school level.

The clarinet still holds an unrivalled position and there are no certain explanations as to why this should be so. We can, of course, make suppositions that the relative cost of the instrument is a deciding factor; as might be the ease of transference from one medium to another, (orchestra to wind band to jazz) and particularly its usefulness as a stepping-stone to the saxophones. But surprisingly, the instrument, unlike the flute, has no champion with whom the majority of children can identify, notwithstanding Jack Brymer and others who would be unheard of by the majority of today's children.

The reasons for such a boom are problematic and there are obviously a good many more theories that need to be considered other than those already cited. Three things are clear however; first, that given the increasing instrumental activity, a disproportionate number of players are wind and brass players; secondly, that the upsurge is particularly noticeable amongst clarinettists and flautists; and thirdly, that such players will need to be included in worthwhile and meaningful ensembles.

Davies (1972), bearing in mind the then present emphasis on wind playing in education, called for some form of wind band but he added that confusion existed as to what constituted a wind band; a similar confusion is abroad today. Emerson's two concise booklets *Ideas for Wind Orchestras* (1972) and *More Ideas for Wind Orchestras* (1975) offered hard-hitting advice on organisation together with a list of repertoire suggestions, and Carlton (*Music in Education*, 1978) pointed out that, although the number of wind bands had increased to the extent that most secondary schools organised a wind group of some kind, the medium was still under-exploited. Light (*Music in Education*, 1978) proffered advice on starting and developing the band whilst Dillon (*Music in Education*, 1978) considered the concert band in school and

music centre and this led to a lively exchange of letters in the columns of
Music in Education (vol. 42, June 1978). ILEA (*Instrumental Teaching*,
London, 1972) stressed the practicality of the wind band and posed the
question:

> outside of strings, what is the instrumental picture of the average musi-
> cally inclined school or college of today? There will be numerous
> clarinets, some flutes and saxophones, the occasional oboe and bassoon,
> many trumpets and a few horns, trombones and drums. This is exactly
> what a Concert Band consists of . . . (pp. 55–6).

Sweby in *Brass Bands in the 20th Century* (V. and G. Brand, eds.,
Egon Publishers, 1979) who was for many years secretary of the
National Schools Brass Band Association, suggested that because of:

> the increasing number of wind bands in schools, . . . a need may exist for
> an association able to do for these bands what has been done for brass
> bands. Present needs of bands which use brass and woodwind are not dis-
> similar to those of school brass bands nearly thirty years ago (p. 172).

Since then the NSBBA has opened its doors to wind bands and, accordingly, dropped the word 'brass' from its title, preferring to be known
simply as the National School Band Association. This change in the constitution has led to increased membership and the Association now aims
to 'foster an interest in music through the playing of brass and woodwind
instruments and the formation of brass and wind bands in schools' (Constitution of the National School Band Association, Summer 1980).

The Military and Concert Band Association had already gone part of
the way to representing the interests of wind bands regionally, although
it was only in its teens when it was subsumed under a larger national
body. The earlier association was formed in 1968 by a group of amateur
bandsmen in the Manchester area to develop links between wind bands.
Although initially only four local bands massed for an annual concert, in
1972 the membership had increased to include bands from the Mid-
lands, South Wales and South West England. In addition to this there
were, and are today, courses organised by the British Youth Wind
Orchestra and the National Wind Band of Scotland.

The British Youth Wind Orchestra was founded by Eric McGavin in
1968, when, sponsored by Boosey & Hawkes, the Schools Music
Association ran an orchestral course for wind players at Westhill
College in Birmingham. The aims of the BYWO are clearly defined: to
provide 'orchestral' experience for some of the large number of young
woodwind and brass players. Accordingly, an orchestral approach to
style and interpretation is favoured.

The Scots, less preoccupied with following in the footsteps of the symphony orchestra, chose to leave the word 'orchestra' out of their title.

Formed in 1972 under the auspices of the Scottish Amateur Music Association, the NWBS meets each summer along with a reserve band. Members of the band are selected after stringent auditions held by the director, Wallace Berry, by visiting many areas of Scotland annually. Applicants are required to be of Grade 8 Associated Board (or equivalent) standard, and several members already hold diplomas. Since the first course Lt. Col. Rodney Bashford has been the band's principal conductor (Wallace Berry being resident conductor).

The country's first advanced diploma in band musicianship was awarded to six students at Salford College of Technology in 1978. In 1980 the first overseas student completed this three-year full-time course, a course pioneered by the Department of Humanities at Salford. For years the conservatoires have given tacit acceptance to the medium by awarding diplomas in military bandmastership, taken traditionally by aspiring bandsmen from Kneller Hall and the Services generally, but the Salford diploma in band musicianship, was the first full-time course of its kind. A diploma course at Leeds College of Music – incorporating brass, wind and modern popular music – has been in existence for some time. More recently, Huddersfield Technical College has offered a preparatory course and an external diploma course, both full-time, in bandsmanship.

Another watershed in instrumental music occurred as a result of the Gulbenkian report of 1978; this was the establishment of the National Centre for Orchestral Studies which provides a bridge from college to professional level. A similar development has taken place at the Royal Northern College in Manchester, and one can also take a higher degree, the Mus. M. in performance. Taylor in *Music Now* (Open University, 1979, p. 81) notes that 'instrumental performance as an integral part of the university curriculum is now generally emphasized' but, unlike the Julliard School and many of the American conservatoires and universities, in this country it is not yet possible to take a doctorate in performance. At school level we have seen a shift to more performance-based 'O' and 'A' levels, most notably in the 'double' London syllabus and that of the Associated Examining Board.

The impact of the media on the minds of children is considerable. On television there have been nationally networked competitions such as Young Musician of the Year and Best of Brass – formerly Champion Brass. On radio there are three nationally broadcast band programmes every week, in addition to many others produced by local stations. There are currently seven journals devoted to brass and wind bands of one type or another, and at least one instrument manufacturer distributes its own 'give-away' magazine to prospective customers. Judging by the number of festivals and competitions currently being held throughout the country, the marching band is enjoying great popularity, though perhaps more for its 'show-biz' than musical appeal. There is even an international conductors' competition for conductors of wind and brass bands, held as part of the World Music Contest in Kerkrade, The Netherlands, every four years. But we must not forget that the opportunities for instrumental work would have been severely restricted without 'hire and buy' schemes, and if musical instrument manufacturers, many overseas, had not made relatively cheap student model instruments.

To cater for the increase in wind music sales, several British publishing houses are distributing American music through franchise and one long-time publisher of brass band music has entered the wind band market for the first time, as well as tailoring scores for British requirements from an established American catalogue. There is even one supplier/publisher that specialises solely in wind music.

With the exception of Gordon Jacob and Stephen Dodgson, few British composers have shown interest in writing for wind band, though things are changing, albeit slowly. An exhibition of British Youth Wind Orchestra commissions, held in 1980 at the British Music Information Centre, revealed relatively unknown works by Gordon Jacob, Wilfred Josephs and David Morgan. 1980 also saw the first London performance of Khachaturian's *The Battle of Stalingrad* given by the Marlborough College Wind Band conducted by Robert Peel; and a new work, *Symphony for Wind Band* by Anthony Milner, which was given its first British performance at the Festival of Wind Instruments at the Royal Northern College of Music.

The wind band's recent past is encouraging for the future, yet there are four interrelated issues which need to be considered if it is to warrant serious, wider acceptance. Firstly, wind bands should go their own way rather than be regarded as a poor man's symphony orchestra. At the same time they need to establish a national identity instead of settling for a mid-atlantic image. Secondly, more composers need to be encouraged to write for wind band. Hitherto, this has been left to the BYWO, the NWBS, of late the BASBWE (which we discuss later) and, occasionally, county authority youth bands, but there is a growing need for new works scored for flexible instrumentation and suitable for school and small mixed wind ensembles. One way of promoting such music would be through a commercially sponsored composition forum. Thirdly, really a corollary to the second issue, publishers ought to ask composers to write under contract for bands, as some did with the brass band, rather than relying on distributing imports. Fourthly, one of the constant criticisms levelled against wind bands is that the players have little opportunity for pursuing their playing after leaving school. In the past, it has not been possible to ride out this particular criticism as the rapid increase in wind bands was brought about mainly at school and music centre level, as distinct from the community in general. Being a school-orientated activity, there was simply little need to form adult bands.

Whilst not wishing to gloss over the problem, the extent of the activity today would indicate that adult bands will develop in step with needs, despite being slow off the mark. Ultimately this has to happen if the wind band is to withstand the test of time. Interestingly, one formerly defunct military band, the Surrey Yeomanry, has come back into existence on an amateur basis through the efforts of young players (the products of youth bands and orchestras). Another newly-formed group, the North West Wind Society, looks to the needs of wind players, adults and children, by promoting recitals and master classes, but best serves its members by organising concerts which include items in which everyone can join, the elementary parts being provided by the society. Societies and organisations instigated to further the cause of wind bands generally have, then, already emerged, none so rapidly as in the case of two associations, known simply by their acronyms, WASBE and BASBWE.

Both the World Association for Symphonic Bands and Ensembles and the British Association for Symphonic Bands and Wind Ensembles came into being as a consequence of the First International Conference which was held in Manchester in 1981. Both are pledged to establish the wind ensemble as a serious and distinctive medium. The first national conference was held in Oxford in 1982: the first world conference in Skien, Norway in 1983.

The conferences have comprised a diversity of activity: concerts, 'clinics', workshops, pre-concert talks given by composers whose works were being performed, illustrated lectures, regional/national panel discussions, open rehearsals, trade exhibitions, and – between the programmed events – a chance to meet confrères and exchange views. Throughout the conferences, delegates have been able to take advantage of resource banks comprising books, journals and repertoire lists, together with record and tape listening facilities.

BASBWE and WASBE are in all essentials what the wind movement has sorely needed. Against their considerable achievements has to be set the task for the future: to incorporate the medium within the mainstream of music or forfeit any claim it has to being a major new force. It would be easy for them to be overawed by the enormity of the task. There is much to be done to create the necessary conditions. There are still many practical difficulties to be worked out: these after all are only the early years of the two associations. But we are left with the distinct impression that the winds are changing.

2 Rationale: why bands in school and music centre?

It is doubtful whether John Hullah Brown would ever have been won over to wind bands. Writing in *Instrumental Music in Schools* (Pitman, 1938), he said:

> Within the scope of an educational system and the limitations of the senior and higher schools, there is no place for the results and effects which would accrue from boys and girls of this age playing any of the orchestral woodwind or brass instruments (p. 23).

One wonders what he would have made of the instrumental activity of the 1980s, though to be fair some of the issues he raised would find validity today. Amongst these there is a particularly interesting dichotomy. Whilst strongly recommending junior brass bands he appears to have been anxious to steer teachers back to the straight and narrow of the violin bow:

> I personally recommend that no wind instruments be included in Senior school work as adjuncts to the string orchestra (which is a complete ensemble in itself), unless a recognised wind combination is a feasible proposition as a unit within itself (p. 24).

His remark in parentheses is unassailable yet in the latter part of the statement he appears to be changing tack. The idea of keeping separate the two ensembles implies the creation of wind bands. Later, Hullah Brown argues that strings and wind should be kept separate on 'artistic' grounds. Clearly his standpoint was one of concern for aesthetic values.

More recently the arguments expressed for wind bands and brass bands in school and music centre have emphasised not so much the artistic but rather the practical aspects, though it will later be argued that the aesthetic appeal is significant, but either unrecognised or fought shy of. For the moment we might take a brief look at some of the arguments which have concentrated on the practical aspects.

Some have stressed the usefulness of the band to the local community as shown by the following comment from a letter by S. Dillon published in *Music in Education*, vol. 42, June 1978:

A school band is a social and community phenomenon: it must take its place in the life of both school and community (p. 239).

Malcolm Carlton drew attention to the possibility of community performances:

The wind band provides a direct route for projecting music within the school at large, and for fulfilling a role in community service by performing at informal public functions as, for example, in the local shopping centre on Saturdays (*Music in Education*, 1978, p. 116).

These are interesting points although the idea is far from new. It is clear from Hardy's *The Mayor of Casterbridge* that the town band was very much a part of the life of small communities. In the novel the band is used to re-introduce the now prosperous Henchard:

A few score yards brought them to the spot where the town band was now shaking the window-panes with the strains of 'The Roast Beef of Old England'.
The building before whose doors they had pitched their music-stands was the chief hotel in Casterbridge – namely the King's Arms.

Whilst acknowledging the importance of music within a social setting and recognising the value of informal performances, we would not seriously suggest building a rationale solely on this. Here we can learn a valuable lesson from our American counterparts some of whom appear to be almost totally subservient to the demands of the community:

. . . the band is a fine public relations medium for the school, its halftime shows often outshining the performance of the football team. Such extrinsic outcomes are not to be discounted. Unfortunately, however, these secondary values often have been used as the sole justification for including large music organisations in the secondary school curriculum (L.W. Edwards and A.D. Katterjohn, *Music Educators Journal*, 1976, p. 53).

Many Americans would maintain that the success of the High School Band at providing half-time entertainment has led to half-time music education. Nowadays communities require all manner of music and musicians, from mobile discothèque units to church organists. A rationale for the band in school must be based on secure educational reasoning. Though the band's usefulness to the community is noteworthy it is not in itself a sufficient rationale for an educationally-based band. There are further considerations.

Perhaps the most pressing reason for including a band in a range of musical activities, is to provide an opportunity for surplus wind and brass instrumentalists prevalent in today's schools. Circumstantial evidence suggests an inverse relationship between the number of flautists and clarinettists and the number of opportunities for them to participate in ensemble work. This surfeit cannot possibly be catered for in the conventional school or music centre orchestra which, apart from a select few wind and brass players, relies on a predominance of strings. Moreover, wind and brass players would spend more playing time in bands than they would normally do sitting in an orchestra. Although these appear to be the reasons uppermost in the minds of music teachers when asked why they include a band within school activities, we should question them. Would we seriously suggest that bands proliferate to 'soak-up' the overproduction of flautists, clarinettists, cornettists and trombonists? Those of us who are involved with schools know how, in the hurly-burly of running a music department, it is all too easy to formulate partially a rationale and confuse cause and effect. Although many school bands were originally formed to solve the problem of involving large numbers of wind and brass players, in practice they may aggravate it by attracting more. Whilst this is, to some extent, inevitable if the band is successful it is necessary to consider the consequences of what we are doing; perhaps perpetuating a constant stream of wind and brass players whose only ensemble experience will be that of playing in bands.

Successful music-making, in whatever form, will always attract further potential players. The important issue here is not that these wind players may have been violinists or pianists, but that they might never before have found a point of contact with music, never have known what it is to be involved in making music with other people.

Music encompasses a myriad of activities. Its points of contact with the life of the individual and community are innumerable. The relevance of a particular musical activity will differ from one situation to another depending on a whole variety of factors including tradition and personal interest.

Bands have a sound, an identity and a unique pull of their own. People are attracted to them because they are a medium of expression in their own right. To believe otherwise is not only to misconstrue the band's function but fundamentally, to fail to realise its unique character and aesthetic appeal.

So far considerable space has been taken to deal with issues some of which are either unconvincing or insufficient in themselves to form adequate foundations for a rationale. Let us turn our attention to an alternative basis for a rationale built not on the band's usefulness to the community or on its effectiveness in soaking up extra wind and brass players, but on the band as a medium of expression in its own right.

The repertoire is wide and can therefore offer unrivalled stylistic contrast from learning to double-dot the *Royal Fireworks Music* to playing *Basin Street Blues* with a Louis Armstrong twelve-eight 'swing' rather than the notated four. Because of the cross-cultural nature of the repertoire, early pieces can be within the culture the children know: later pieces beyond this. There is, to some extent, a natural progression of skills. Inexperienced players can be introduced into the band by playing third clarinet/cornet parts and gradually move up the band as their musicianship increases. Further, group teaching becomes practicable because of the similarity of fingering patterns and homogeneity within the two families of instruments, woodwind and brass. One publisher has even designed a group teaching method for full band. Interestingly, Swanwick (*Classical Music*, 1979, p. 21) writing on group teaching, cites the example of an American High School band in which 'people learn much of playing technique and stylistic understanding from the group itself.'

Naturally, we are not thinking of an activity whose product can be assessed solely by its performances – these can too easily paper over the cracks in the process fabric – but of an activity on a musical rather than mechanical level in which judgement and discrimination are developed in tandem with manipulative instrumental skills. Providing we pay attention to the players' musical education as a whole, rather than train them merely as bandsmen, the band can prove a musically satisfying ensemble capable of sensitivity and great expression. Quantz's tutor of 1752, *The Art of Flute Playing*, makes clear that the author was not interested merely in teaching dexterous finger work, but rather in making his pupils all-round musicians. Failure to do this could result in what Swanwick terms 'instrumental operatives':

> One American student told me that she stopped playing the clarinet after thirteen years of being in a school band. She had never liked the sound of the instrument! Is this music education, or is it more like a training as an instrumental operative? (*Music Teacher*, 1978, p.17)

Unfortunately this is all too common with many so-called 'successful' bands. The disparity between the image of the band in concert and reality of the rehearsal is often quite significant. A form of tunnel vision sets in whereby, losing sight of everything else, the pursuit of lofty goals, spurred on by increasingly large and more prestigious performances, goes on unabashed by a falling-off of all-round musicianship and without regard to more intrinsic qualities. Such practice has a stultifying effect on music and represents a completely different way of working from the one we are proposing. If we are so rigid and inflexible that we cannot adapt to changing circumstances, the activity becomes mechanical and inhuman. In contrast, if we have in our minds certain criteria, or principles of judgement, which are broad enough to allow for players' developing needs and abilities, and if we take time not merely to point out musical details but also to make the rehearsals a musical experience, it is possible to create an atmosphere which is conducive to critical listening and to the development of all-round musicianship. In these circumstances performance is seen as an adjunct to learning, not the reverse.

Finally, sometimes, when asking a headmaster, advisor or PTA for assistance with the cost of purchasing instruments, we need to justify the band in school. In these circumstances the following statement could prove useful:

A band is a versatile ensemble which can equip its members with the techniques and practices required in a variety of musical styles and idioms. The sound and the appeal of a band are unique. It can be a musically satisfying medium capable of engendering great sensitivity in players.

Part II CLASS BAND

3   The class band

Instrumental music within the curriculum

Whatever extra-curricular activities flourish in school, commitment to educating everyone must be unceasing. As a general practitioner, the school music teacher's time is at a premium, for in addition to his rôle as educator, he is expected to administer visiting instrumental teachers, organise extra-curricular rehearsals for orchestras, choirs and bands, not to mention productions. The energy required to sustain this game of musical chairs is substantial. Horton makes the point that in maintained schools the person taking class music often doubles as Director of Music and that, 'we shall have to look very, very closely at this and watch the strain on our teachers' (quoted in G. Brace, *Music and the Secondary School Timetable*, University of Exeter Institute of Education (1970), p. 11).

We could argue a strong case for employing a teacher to take charge of the so-called extra-curricular activities, as in the public schools, and to work hours other than the normal school day, although strong support from the children would be unlikely to develop without the necessary day-to-day contact within the classroom. In any case, such an appointment is hardly viable in today's economic climate.

Often it is because of the accommodating attitude of music staff that many of the orchestras, bands and choirs function at all. It is almost an unwritten agreement on securing a post as a music teacher that you are prepared to spend time and energy outside of the classroom. If we are to continue in these dual rôles then it would seem logical to try to bring them more in line with each other and, whilst classroom practice can influence the extra-curricular activities, it is conceivable that the reverse may also be true.

We should consider the possibilities of including within the curriculum what are commonly referred to as extra-curricular (but more precisely are extra-timetabled) rehearsals; it is important to distinguish between the two.

The term extra-curricular is a misnomer, at best it has a rather

20

restricted meaning. It implies leisure-time activities of secondary importance to curricular work, and not worthy of a place on the school timetable. Even by this reading of the term, it is hardly extra-curricular to the work of a music department but it is vital to the needs of its students. Tagged on to what are commonly overfull days, so-called extra-curricular activities make excessive demands on the students' attention span and powers of concentration, and even greater demands on the teachers' physical and mental stamina. Teachers have extended their contact time without question, committing themselves to a regular pattern of long working days. For all intents and purposes elective activities might as well be added to the school timetable – they are added as required activities to the music teacher's.

Apart from re-examining curricular and extra-curricular music, we should look again at the instruments we use in each setting. Those of the Orff variety based on the gamelan rather than symphonic orchestra have been called 'classroom instruments'. By choosing carefully and making sure that 'real' instruments are included, erring on the side of buying larger rather than smaller untuned percussion, we stay clear of jibes that we are playing about with 'toys' or that we are using specially produced classroom instruments. Not only does the work assume a more professional level but also the instruments are durable and useful with the school orchestra or band. Moreover we should be encouraging the children who have instrumental lessons (our already competent players) to play, improvise and assist in class.

Classroom activities

The classroom ensemble may be termed a 'class band', irrespective of the type of instruments brought to the lessons. These could include strings, brass, wind and guitars, along with piano accordion and others. The term 'class band' is more acceptable to the adolescent than 'classroom orchestra'. The term is general, denoting a collection of almost any instruments. We refer to the brass band, the wind band, the dance band and even the rock band, which in many ways has superseded the word 'group' in the world of pop. The all-inclusive quality of the term suits the *ad hoc* collection and ever-changing instrumentation. Even if it is fashionable to use such a term, then it is better to go with the prevailing trend and become more relevant to the outside world and media.

As already stated, the instruments should be 'real' and professional. Apart from personal instruments brought to the lessons, a basic ensemble is essential for a satisfactory sound. As well as the customary piano (used, of course, to fill in harmonies and which should be dispensed with whenever possible), the drum kit is most useful both complete and split up around the class. In the eyes of the adolescent the kit certainly quells the 'playing about with toys' theory. It is as well to have the kit close at hand, to keep strict control of the beat and to dampen over-enthusiastic drummers. If the room is carpeted the sound will be more like that of the studio, if not, a blanket in the bass drum or a gym mat placed under the kit will soften a certain amount of boom. Other untuned percussion instruments can of course, be added but again the larger the better. Strangely enough, the Brazilian tambourine (without head) is far more acceptable than those with heads which tend to be associated with the Salvation Army or junior school music and move-ment classes. Bongos prove very appealing but are better with a stand, particularly when given to girls. Most on the market today have plastic heads and sound better played with soft sticks in all but expert hands.

Example 1 is a collection of pieces for drum kit and untuned per-cussion. The pieces can be used as a basis for improvisation using guitars, chord or melodic instruments, or as pieces in their own right. The written notation need not be strictly adhered to but is meant as a guide to rhythmic possibilities. All the parts may be taught by rote and the kit could be played either by one person or split up and played by several. The pieces are not graded because certain rhythms are easier for different people. However, the opening numbers are less intricate and are therefore easily possible with beginners. Many of the rhythms used are already familiar to pupils steeped in the world of pop music. The patterns can be extended by constantly changing the instrumen-tation and thus changing the tone colours. In the early stages where there are hand clapping and foot tapping parts, these should be per-formed by splitting the class into two rather than each student attempt-ing both parts simultaneously (see pages 24–5).

Other instruments used will vary considerably depending on resources and the musical interests of the class. The teacher can hardly be expected to be proficient on all of them but when things go wrong it is useful to know, instantly, not only who is playing the wrong notes but also how to put them right. Action notations tell you quickly about the mechanics of a particular instrument and are helpful. These should be placed at the beginning of the music and not underneath each note or the student may rely upon this rather than the orthodox notation. Even if the class is not using notation it will assist the teacher in knowing what will work (see page 26).

Kendor Music (USA) publish a series called 'Ensembles Without Instruments', reminiscent of Orff-Schulwerk. These rhythmic pieces require hand clapping, finger snapping, foot tapping and knee slapping (one's own!) and can be done with large classes. There are also interesting canonic rhythms for group use in 'The Music Group' *Book 1* by John Horton (Schott), again an Orff idea.

Nowadays, electronics are pervading many aspects of music. There has been a tremendous growth industry of electronic organs for home use and many of the smaller ones are now being brought into the classroom. The smaller synthesizers are within reach of many music departments and can be invaluable. Played by an elementary pianist they can double as a bass instrument (an instrument which is at a premium in the classroom). Many electric pianos, even the inexpensive ones, have the facility to imitate a bass guitar and can be useful for providing ostinati. They are cheaper and probably more useful than the bass xylophone.

Ostinati and percussion accompaniments work well and the more able instrumentalists can be encouraged to improvise or compose over them. The tunes in example 2 have ostinati, pedal points, or recurring bass patterns usually over a two-bar phrase. They can be used in a variety of ways, either by themselves or with melodies, as a basis for improvisation, or recorded onto a tape loop and played back. In the second of the two examples, chord symbols are included for guitars, chord organs and autoharp (see pages 27–8).

After much rhythmic and ostinato work by rote, the need for notation should have arisen, usually as a result of works becoming too long to remember in detail. At this point notation may be introduced either in the simplified rhythmic form used in *New Sounds in Class* by G. Self (Universal); or in staff form as in *Class in Concert* by W. Salaman (Middle Eight) or *Group Music Making* by M.J. McMurtary (Longman); or by a combination of both as in *Music for Young Players* (Universal).

Example 3 is based on traditional staff notation. It is in the style of one of Satie's *Gymnopédies*. Recorders use left hand only. The guitar part is restricted to open strings and the elementary B flat part, essentially for clarinet, does not go above the break. With the possibility that a variety of transposing instruments will be present, the choice of key favours the recorders and classroom instruments as players of these are likely to be of a lower standard than those on orchestral, wind band, or brass band instruments (see pages 29–30).

Often there may be several particularly competent players in class and for them Example 4 offers a chance for solos either written or extemporised. These players can also be encouraged to make up descants or obbligati (see pages 31–2).

Example 1:

1: Basic Rock Pattern
(♩=100)
Finger Clicks
Foot Tapping
Drums

2: Basic Rock Pattern
(♩=120)
Tambourine
Hand Clapping
Drums

3: A Slow Reggae
(♩=60)
Hand Clapping
Foot Tapping
Drums

4: A Calypso
(♩=100-120)
Hand Clapping (1)
Hand Clapping (2)
Drums

5: A Rock and Roll (to be played as if written in 12/8)
(♩=120)
Hand Clapping (1)
Hand Clapping (2)
Drums

6: A Jazz Waltz (one in a bar)
(♩=60)
Hand Clapping (1)   (2 Bar Phrase)
Finger Clicks (2)
Drums

25

Fingering for new notes:

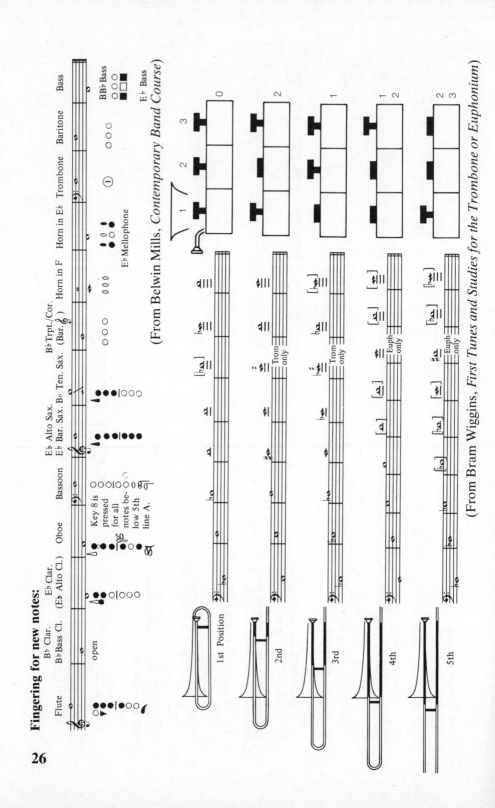

(From Belwin Mills, *Contemporary Band Course*)

(From Bram Wiggins, *First Tunes and Studies for the Trombone or Euphonium*)

26

Example 2a:

Example 2b:

Example 3:

Gymnopédie

Kevin Thompson

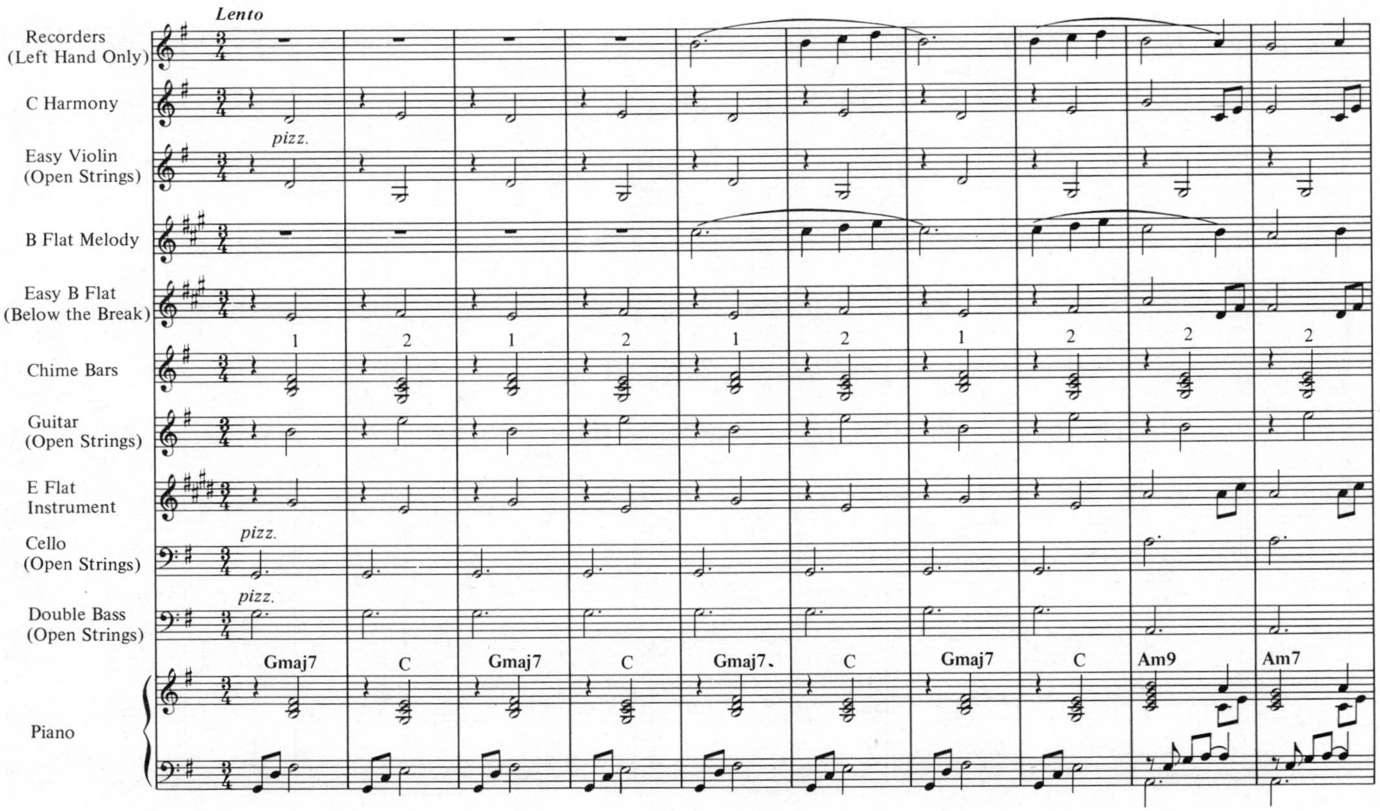

Example 4:

I am a Fine Musician

The entire class plays except where marked solo. Tuned percussion play throughout. Each verse should have a different soloist.

German folk melody

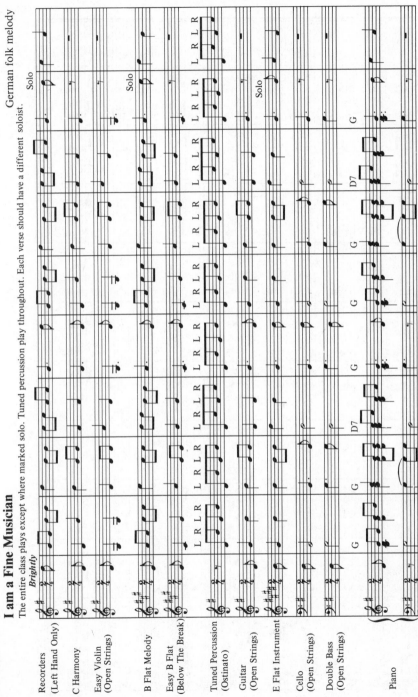

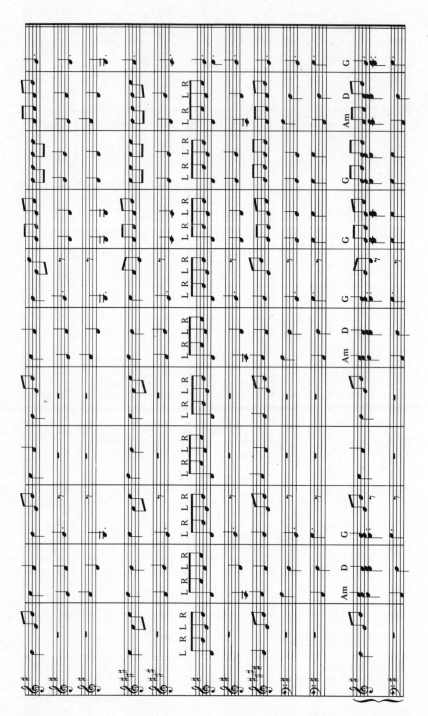

32

4 Writing for specific classes: four examples

A band approach to classroom music will necessarily involve the teacher in tailoring parts for the instrumentalists present. Chapter four focuses on the problems encountered in writing for a wide range of abilities and the sorts of mixed instrumentation found in class. By use of case studies or examples, it suggests ways in which some of the problems might be overcome. Within each of the four classes described there were particular strengths: the first-year class had many singers and recorder players; the second- and third-year classes a wide spread of instrumentalists; the fourth-year students had a certain rhythmic ability. Here then are brief descriptions of the four classes together with the pieces scored for them.

1: First-year class

Many first years arrive at their secondary school with some experience of recorder work. Quite a large cross-section from this first-year class had attended the same junior school where they had pursued a recorder course to some depth. In addition to the recorder players, two girls, Sarah and Vicky, had recently taken up the flute and clarinet respectively. The class teacher was anxious to make use of the skills many of the newly-arrived first-years had already acquired, but most of all wanted to show them that the work covered in their junior school had relevance to that of the secondary school.

In the arrangement of 'Sing' the recorders and flute play an obbligato whilst the singers and clarinet have the tune; the clarinet blending well with voices. The song was arranged yet again for full band and performed by the new-intake recorder players at the autumn term's concert (see pages 34–5).

2: Second-year class

This large second-year class had a very wide range of ability. Within the group there were many members of the choir, three oboists, a French

33

Example 1:

Sing

J. Raposo

horn player, a Salvation Army trombonist who read only treble clef, and a tuba player.

Christopher, an attention-seeker, could be disruptive if he were not allowed to play drums; he regarded most other instruments as childish toys. One of the oboists, Susan, was a competent pianist and in this capacity helped out from time to time. Others alternated between singing and playing either their own or classroom instruments. Generally, it was a musical class and despite Christopher they had a junior school freshness and enthusiasm for the subject.

In the song 'Without You' the piano part has been simplified so that Susan could cope with it. Instead of using all three oboes it uses only one, though often, in class, a second oboe would play the repeat. The trombone takes over the tune at B whilst the horn plays a counter-melody which is later taken up by the trombone. The tuba (really an E flat bass in this case) plays the bass line of the piano part. Even with a player accustomed to reading treble clef, the part need not be transposed provided that the player is using an E flat bass as it uses the same lines and spaces as concert-pitch bass clef:

For years, brass band E flat bass players have read orchestral bass clef parts as treble clef and adjusted the key signature accordingly. Obviously, accidentals will differ. (An A natural bass clef will become an F sharp treble clef.) There is a similar coincidence with tenor clef trombone parts and treble clef trombone parts when transposed for B flat instrument:

In the score, bass clef for the trombone has been used; however, with this particular player the part had to be written in treble clef.

The same song, 'Without You', was rehearsed with another second-year class in which there were two clarinettists. These played the falling third pattern (in the right hand of the piano part) but transposed up a tone for B flat clarinet. It was quite effective to have just the girls singing verse one, boys, verse two and everyone joining in the chorus (see pages 37–9).

3: Third-year class

Example 3 was scored for a third-year special music option class of twenty-two. By the third year many of the instrumentalists were quite

Example 2:

smile, but in your eyes your sorrow   shows,   yes it   shows.   Well, I
on - ly fair that I should let you   know,   let you

know.   I can't live   if   liv-ing is with-out you___. I can't

live   I can't live an-y - more.   I can't live   if liv-ing is without you. I can't

live,   I can't live an-y - more.

proficient and several played more than one instrument. Within the class there were choir members, several recorder players, three clarinettists, a flautist, an E flat tenor horn player, and a bassoonist who was particularly competent.

'Here, There and Everywhere' has some interest for bassoon yet the other parts are easily managed by elementary players. Second and third clarinet parts remain below the break (see pages 41–2).

4: Fourth-year music option

The fourth-year option class led to 'O' level music performance. With this class, greater insight is gained by describing the individuals comprising it, rather than the class as a whole. All the members of the group had come through the practical experiences already detailed. Here then are brief descriptions of the individuals as recounted by their teacher at the time:

> Ian is a self-taught composer and pianist in addition to being the drummer with the band. He has ambitions of becoming a famous pop composer and he spends much of his spare time writing his own songs. He has a natural talent which is rare. His musical education has been from one aural experience to another, collecting records, copying riffs and styles and pursuing a course which is entirely self-directed. Perhaps in some schools where the emphasis was on academic and high culture music, Ian would be regarded as a low brow if he were noticed at all.

> Angela, bespectacled, is an avid reader and precisely the opposite of Ian. She has had some four years' school tuition on the clarinet and she has recently passed grade 8. She is actively involved in school music and leads the wind band. She is regarded by the others as a swot but likeable none the less.

Angela had shown an interest in arranging for the music group and example 4 is a piece she adapted from a piano score. Obviously some of the parts could have been better placed but the arrangement shows more than just a basic knowledge of the instruments and a fair amount of enterprise (see page 43).

> Julie M. is an ex-clarinettist turned tenor saxophone player. She has similar improvisatory skills to Ian and has absolute pitch.

> Jean is principal flautist with the town Youth Symphony Orchestra. Like Angela she has recently gained grade 8 and, reluctantly, grade 4 on the piano.

> Sara, an ex-clarinet player, is teaching herself the alto saxophone.

> Michael W. is a cornet player and a Salvationist.

> Michael S. is a trumpeter whose ambition is to go to Kneller Hall and

Example 3:

Here, There and Everywhere

Lennon & McCartney

Example 4:

Polonaise in G

J.S. Bach (arr. Angela, aged 14)

become an army bandsman. In the school band he doubles on drums from time to time.

Sandra is the middle one of three sisters who have all taken an active part in school music. She plays the clarinet and has a superb voice.

Julie W. is a violinist and very much the academic music student.

Steven is a self-taught drummer who has recently started having trombone lessons.

Philip, a West Indian boy, is a cornet player and has transferred from another school.

Example 5 is more advanced than previous pieces and it exploits the fourth-year's rhythmic ability. This oddly-assorted collection of instruments had no real bass and consequently the tenor saxophone had to fulfil that role. Both saxophone parts are of an elementary standard as is the violin part. Clarinet parts are more complex both rhythmically and technically. Flute, trumpet and cornet parts carry much of the tune. The canonic section requires careful counting and far more independence of movement than previously encountered. The piano part is relatively easy incorporating the ostinato rhythm and tune juxtaposed with arpeggio figures. This part was, of course, dispensed with when the ensemble was complete. The students found little difficulty in swallowing the idiom; there was kudos in performing music in five! (see pages 45–7).

Although the above compositions and arrangements were intended for the specific classes and are progressive, there is no reason why, with some adaptation, they could not be used with others. Of the four classes cited, the effects on the first-year class were perhaps more immediate than the others – the most beneficial effect being that of integrating the new students fully into the work of the secondary school within the formative first term.

Example 5:

Pentad

Kevin Thompson

45

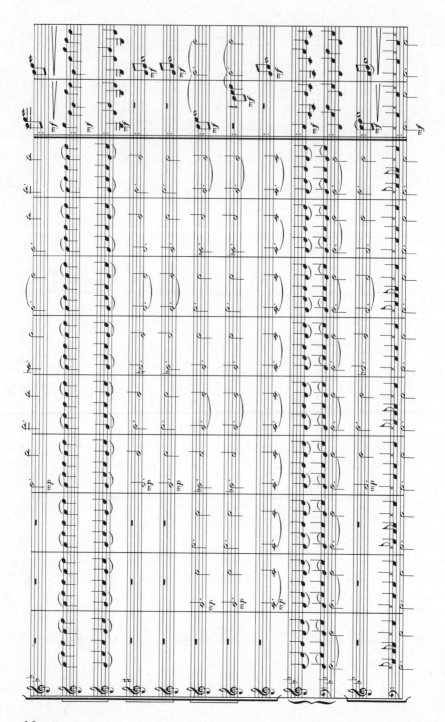

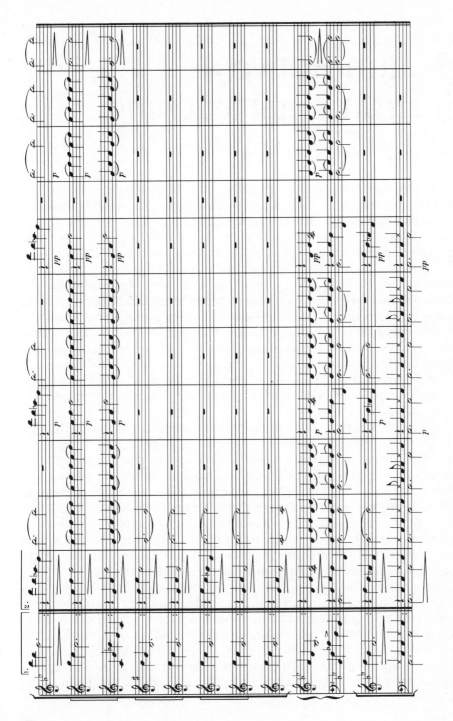

47

5 Innovative instrumental teaching

Two types of activity are especially difficult to accommodate within the school timetable; one is the individual lesson, the other is the large-scale band rehearsal. Music teachers have an unparalleled problem in convening rehearsals within the school day as, unlike games which tend to be based on stratified year-groups, bands tend to draw students from a number of year-groups, and often from the entire age-range of the school. Vertical or family grouping (an arrangement whereby students from within a two or three year age-range are timetabled for music at the same time) makes a mixture of small and large group activity possible: viable ensembles, sectional rehearsals, upper or lower school bands, and group lessons in which younger students can learn in the company of more experienced students. It can also allow for a whole variety of student-directed activities which might include more adventurous permutations and combinations of purpose groups and practice time for the musically involved.

It would hardly be feasible to organise vertical grouping across all years to provide an entire wind band or brass band. Large-scale activities would probably be better catered for at a music centre. Within school, activities would, perforce, be stratified at least into broad age bands, in the way that many large comprehensives are broken down into a number of self-contained upper, lower and middle schools. There may be a junior, elementary string group, spanning years one to three; a middle school wind ensemble, for fourth and fifth formers; and a brass ensemble at sixth form level. In primary schools it is only the age groups seven to eight and nine to ten which need be differentiated.

Programmes for 'shop window' occasions, concerts and carol services could be rehearsed by ready-made ensembles working in a music workshop environment similar to that of the timetabled ensemble lessons at Pimlico School where a complete ensemble training is offered with the necessary regular time allocated to it, or the American School in London where the fourteen performing groups, including four 'grade' (year-group) bands, are each scheduled within the mainstream of the curriculum. It should not simply be a case of preparing frantically towards a fast approaching performance of specially chosen pieces, but a matter of putting on show the everyday work of the students so that they may gain the experience of a public performance. The distinction might appear academic but it is a fundamental one nonetheless. Programmes for concerts should be a logical outgrowth of the music being studied in the curriculum, not an overriding concern towards which everything else is channelled.

An occasional activity might be a 'music in action' workshop: one whole week of intensive music-making involving recitals by visiting ensembles, large and small group playing, demonstrations by professional players and concerts given by experimental groups.

It is important to stress that music would be viewed as an umbrella term like games: resources pooled for greater efficiency; the rôle of instrumental teachers looked at *de novo*; utilisation of class teachers' instrumental skills; and aims and objectives common to instrumental and classroom teachers formulated.

Faced with the sorts of changes envisaged we must ask ourselves a whole range of questions, including for example: How can the two rôles be brought closer together yet quintessentially remain different? How can instrumentalists and classroom teachers break down the present logjam that exists between them? How can they integrate their respective work yet at the same time preserve some of the specialist nature of their rôles? How feasible is integration? Will instrumental teachers be adaptable enough to cope with change, or will it overwhelm them? Could they accept radical changes to instrumental teaching methods, chiefly, that is, teaching groups? Would they relate to the curriculum as a whole?

What is in mind is that the instrumental teacher will enact with equal rigour several interlocking rôles: as consummate musician, having the ability to move widely through the various strands of musical styles and idioms; as group and individual teacher, widening his own teaching range and at ease in large and small-scale teaching situations; as team teacher and leader of team-teaching sessions, working with colleagues in a way that makes for mutual co-operation yet at the same time encourages individual expression; as initiator and practitioner of music curricula, devising learning experiences as an integral part of a total structured curriculum.

Teachers would need to be versatile, more willing to develop catholicity of musical tastes. For example, a foundation course for clarinettists could include demonstrations in a variety of styles from Mozart to traditional and modern jazz and lead on to other instruments, perhaps alto and tenor saxophone. We can be justifiably outraged by the narrowness of modern specialisation, of brass band instrumentalists who cannot be bothered to learn French horn fingering.

Particularly in the sort of pluralistic society which exists today with many possible ways of coming to music, such divisive attitudes compartmentalise music and create artificial barriers when we should be building bridges. Personal preferences towards one brand of music can be taken into account, perhaps when deciding on a range of activities, but they should not intrude. In this way a pupil interested in brass band music may find something else he likes; he will have been exposed to a variety of other mediums. Moreover by exposing him to music he would not have sought out for himself, his horizons will have been expanded. Such learning experiences must offer something immediate but also something longer term that will lead on.

It is not simply a matter of what pupils should know but what they can do with what they know. Such a course would necessarily involve a partnership between instrumental and classroom teachers. The key is partnership. Integration here does not involve junior and senior partners but equals sharing initiative and with an equal say in the spread of activities on offer. The first year of the secondary school would seem to provide a fitting interface.

From a school teaching viewpoint, one of the defects of the Conservatoire system in which a large number of our instrumentalists have undergone initial training, is specialisation at too early a stage. It does not follow, however, that if music college courses were more general, less concerned with a single instrument, a particular area of music, or with the specificities that we are so good at, that our attitudes would necessarily change, but our skills at teaching a range of instruments, in a variety of idioms to a broader base of pupils, might be sharpened. Neither does it follow that to do this would necessarily mean a decline in the standards of instrumental teaching or of performance, nor that larger numbers of pupils would need only simple fare, though it is easy to see such arguments being put forward by those who have as their prime objective the provision of players for the youth wind band or championship brass band. Of course it is possible to be restricted by one's own versatility, the old adage 'Jack of all trades' is true enough, but at all-ability foundation course level it would be necessary to maintain an overview of the subject, not to travel down some narrow, specialised avenue which might only attract a minority. Teachers contributing to this type of early-years course would have to accept a dual rôle, part *animateur* – capable of simplifying for the benefit of a general audience – and part traditional instrumental specialist.

But if the rôle of the instrumental teacher becomes broader, more like that of the classroom music teacher (a general practitioner) where is the dividing line between the two to be drawn? Is the short answer that it becomes blurred and in reality ceases to exist? The questions highlight a dilemma that faces us: on the one hand we want to continue to enjoy the diversity of musical expertise that an instrumental team can offer and the benefits that accrue, that is youth wind bands and brass bands of remarkable quality; on the other hand, we want instrumental teachers to concern themselves more with education, for their work to be integrated into the curriculum and into the school as a whole, to think of themselves as teachers as well as musicians. Emphatically, the instrumental teacher should not be squeezed out of the system, as appears to be the case in some quarters, thought of as an expendable luxury that we can no longer afford, but brought into the classroom.

To indicate further the place of instrumental music within the curriculum, three scenarios are delineated in detail: two instrumental lessons, in turn woodwind and brass; and thirdly, a rehearsal which differs from the traditional type in respect to student activities. It is envisaged, and indeed emphasised, that each of the activities set out would form part of a comprehensive course reaching all pupils, offering all the opportunity to participate at a variety of levels. From time to time individuals may be taken out of the seedbed to be given booster lessons or to make up groups of high achievers. The scenarios are not intended to be taken as exemplary models of how to proceed; they merely demonstrate possible lines of approach and invite consideration on that basis.

Scenario 1

A woodwind group of eight, comprising four flautists and four clarinettists, spends a considerable amount of time readjusting mouthpieces, reeds and ligatures. After attending studiously to each player's embouchure, the teacher asks if anyone can recall the rhythmic pattern they made up last time. Some of the players remember and are able to demonstrate their answers. Turning to *Woodwind Workbook* (Novello) by Philippe Oboussier, they play their own rhythmic patterns, flautists first on the flute head (sounding A flat) and then clarinettists on the mouthpiece and barrel of the instruments (sounding F). Subsequently, they play the minor third as a chord, then each player in turn improvises a new rhythm. After every improvisation the chord is restated and the group repeats the given pattern. Eventually, the simple memory game gives way to increasingly complex variants: the patterns are played backwards, dynamics are alternated and different tonguing syllables are used. When the instruments are fully assembled and checked for alignment by the teacher, the players profitably spend time matching tones, listening for flatness or sharpness, separating and combining interesting sounds.

Scenario 2

In a room away from the rest of the school, a group of eight aspiring brass players are struggling to play open Gs and Cs at the same time. As often happens through attributes either innate or developed, two of the group have already some semblance of embouchure; what the others lack in aptitude they make up for in perseverance. The 'naturals' are allotted the upper notes of a four-part chord whilst the rest, two on each part, are given the lower notes. Each pair first sings then plays its respective notes. Eventually a complete if not resounding chord is managed. After some guidance from the teacher on production, the composition *Swell Piece* by James Tenney is introduced:

Swell Piece for Alison Knowles

James Tenney

To be performed by any number of instruments beyond three, and lasting any length of time previously agreed upon.

Each performer plays one long tone after another (actual durations and pitches free and independent).

Each tone begins as softly as possible, builds up to maximum intensity, then fades away into (individual) silence.

Within each tone, as little change of pitch or timbre as possible, in spite of the intensity changes.

James Tenney 12/67

The players carefully read the directions for themselves and then discuss how they might achieve a climactic performance. Two contrasting instrumental choirs are formed, one made up of bright (cylindrical) tones, the other of mellow (conical) tones. After a reminder to take care of the instruments, one of the groups is sent off to practise in another room. The teacher first stays behind to help one group, then looks in to see how the other group is progressing. In addition to identifying individual problems, the teacher relays those that have repercussions for the whole class.

The players of larger instruments – euphonium and tuba – find it difficult and taxing to build the required intensity of dynamic so have to work towards softer, more subtle beginnings. Both groups show concern for the tone quality, timbre and character of the music they are attempting to create. They look discerningly at the overall structure, decide who will play when, who will begin, who will finish the piece. They work on building sound layers, contrasting antiphonal colour changes, fading one sound out and blending another in. They discover and practise techniques for producing the sounds such as breath control, steadiness of stance, tonguing actions required to start and complete each note.

After forty minutes or so the two groups come together again to perform their pieces. Both are recorded on to tape. Not surprisingly, even though the groups have held the directions in mind, the pieces are undoubtedly dissimilar in character and intention, though both have sensitive, imaginative moments. Of course there are many unplanned moments too, but that is only to be expected with such inexperienced players, grappling with newly-acquired techniques. Listening again to the performances, the players make constructive comments about the pieces and decide when it is necessary to play in this way. As an unsought by-product, they have alighted on skills vital to any brass player. The teacher chooses to conclude the lesson by playing a recording of *Sonata Pian' e Forte* by Giovanni Gabrieli.

Scenario 3

After following a standard course for beginner band in which much of the playing has been unison and massed – albeit in small groups – the players want to tackle, collectively in ensemble, something more imaginative and possibly of more intrinsic value. *Sculpture* from *Stone Images* by Sidney Hodkinson is an attempt to fuse basic instrumental playing with contemporary compositional technique. Moreover, it shifts the emphasis from skill learning towards aural awareness and ordering of sounds.

Each of the instrumental parts, written within a restricted compass, makes few technical demands. In this way, the restrictions (imposed for essentially practical reasons) allow the players to focus their attention on changing texture, sharpening dynamics and contrasting ensemble timbre. Each of the players is allocated one note only to play during each of the four movements. As the number of parts is arbitrary, there is substantial latitude in respect to the instrumental line-up, so much so that the piece is playable by almost any *ad hoc* ensemble. The teacher then is free to assign the parts at his discretion and according to the individual potential of the players on hand. In effect, each player, or group

Sculpture

a study in crescendo/diminuendo
Sidney Hodkinson

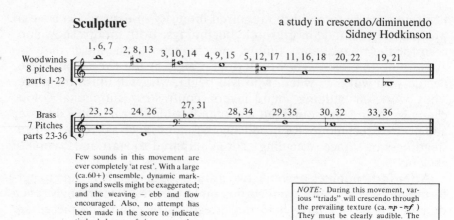

Few sounds in this movement are ever completely 'at rest'. With a large (ca.60+) ensemble, dynamic markings and swells might be exaggerated; and the weaving – ebb and flow encouraged. Also, no attempt has been made in the score to indicate timbral changes of given notes; they are constant throughout.

NOTE: During this movement, various "triads" will crescendo through the prevailing texture (ca. *mp – mf*) They must be clearly audible. The circled black notes are simply an aural guide for the conductor.

of players, has solo or soli notes. Three symbols are used throughout to indicate how the notes should be played:

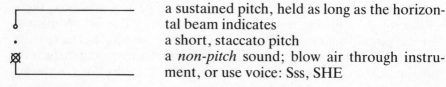

a sustained pitch, held as long as the horizontal beam indicates
a short, staccato pitch
a *non-pitch* sound; blow air through instrument, or use voice: Sss, SHE

Note lengths are approximate. Entrances and exits are made according to the place indicated in the score between the leader's downbeats.

Sidney Hodkinson suggests that, prior to playing, the players briefly discuss the symbolism of the megaliths portrayed and the need for some form of appropriate notation for the sounds they evoke. Further, he suggests that the players listen to recordings of works exemplifying contemporary styles of composition: Boulez, Ligeti, Penderecki, Reich and Xenakis are mentioned amongst others.

Rehearsals begin in small groups with pupils taking turns at conducting. The groups are set apart in different areas of the school hall so that spatial and antiphonal effects can be added. The performance is recorded in order that the players can discuss further the composer's intention in setting down the music. The work is then taken as a starting-point for improvisation and composition with similar limitations. Players find that such restrictions challenge, stimulate and channel their creative thoughts.

The composition of each type of group deviates according to whether a particular piece requires more or fewer instruments. Tone quality is imitated, stylistic conventions emulated, interpretation discussed, rhythms copied and structural points noted. The quality of the work hinges largely on the musical judgement of the students, as well as on the ability of the teacher to formulate attainable goals. Encouragement and criticism play key rôles. The activities encompass experimentation, listening and observing. Except for 'sound' (the only real criterion), the absence of rules makes many more demands of the participants.

Part III WIND BAND

6 An introduction

Nowadays, wind bands come in all shapes and sizes from octets performing eighteenth-century *harmonie* to ensembles of over a hundred. There are 'symphonic wind' bands, 'concert' bands and 'marching' bands to name but a few, as well as various hybrids which have their own peculiar nomenclature. This bewildering state of affairs is further compounded by bands' conflicting tastes and interests, and so a brief comparative look at the main types of wind, brass and percussion combinations may prove helpful.

The symphonic wind band, or wind orchestra (the title generally preferred in Britain) denotes an orchestral approach. The repertoire tends to be more European in origin than other types of band, although many of the arrangements are by Americans. Speaking generally, symphonic wind band music favours flutes, oboes and bassoons. The playing is generally restrained and the scoring transparent. In transcriptions – alas, we do not yet share the American fondness for original music – clarinets take on the string parts and the brass are assigned to their normal incisive orchestral rôle. British groups have been markedly reluctant to adopt the wind ensemble ideal of one player per part, so symphonic wind bands, or wind orchestras, remain bands and not wind ensembles.

Notably unimpeded by anything in the way of excess weight or clutter, the medium of the 'wind ensemble', characterised by a combination of flexible instrumentation and one player per part, is ideally attuned to a programme comprising, say, Stravinsky's *Concerto for Piano and Wind* and Holst's *Hammersmith*. The format of the ensemble is based on the ideas, outlined previously, of Frederick Fennell. Should wind ensembles be heard more frequently in this country, a few wind conductors might doubt the efficacy of large bands in which some players may become mere ciphers. Why, in our eagerness to involve everyone, should we feel it necessary (at advanced level) to occupy all players at all times?

As one would expect, the title 'concert' band (like concert orchestra) implies a repertoire of a lighter nature, although the instrumentation does not preclude more serious works. Similar instrumentation is used by the British 'military' band which, despite the full regimental massed bands we hear on the march, is quite a modest-sized affair.

Conversely, the 'marching' band, (another transatlantic phenomenon) is a very large ensemble which developed out of the military band in the early twenties. Essentially intended for outdoor and on the march performances, its *raison d'être* appears to be half-time entertainment at football games. Consequently, the instruments used (which are mostly forward facing) are chosen for their carrying power and march suitability; hence the absence of the double reeds – oboes and bassoons. French horns are particularly susceptible to weather changes because of their rotary valves so the E flat horn is preferred. Bands of this type spend as much time practising intricate marching patterns as they do music; it is easy to see why. It would be heartening to believe that such players might go on to more musically stimulating ends. It seems perverse to deprecate this type of ensemble as it obviously fulfils a need and pitches its performances accordingly. The recent upsurge of interest in marching bands in this country is testimony to this. But then the last decade or so has been especially significant in establishing all manner of wind bands in schools and music centres.

Music centre or borough bands, made up of players from a variety of schools within a particular locality, exist throughout the country. In many authorities they function in addition to, and in some instances in place of, school bands. Music centre wind bands are generally larger ensembles than those found in schools, and more able to afford the rarer, expensive instruments. Consequently they have an extended range of colour and timbre, with the potential to perform both large- and small-scale works. By the same token, this type of band may well be less than satisfactory as its size can often prevent the expression of musicality and rehearsals may become subject to massed regimentation.

7 Putting them together

A starting place for the beginner band may be the mixed ensemble. In some cases a band has gradually evolved from a larger, mixed ensemble possibly through the desire of the teacher to stretch the more able brass and wind players. It is likely that some schools will, either through force of circumstance or choice, want to keep strings and recorders playing with the wind band – and why not? Even if the title is 'wind band', which for some is axiomatic despite the percussion section, a band need not be an all or nothing proposition. Some (particularly junior) schools will choose to add to the majority of wind and brass almost any instrument to hand. (Traditional wind band devotees will now be totally nonplussed by this idea.) The primary consideration must be for a well-balanced, pleasant-sounding ensemble. In some schools cellos provide a much needed bass line to an otherwise top-heavy band: these are effective and contribute to the overall balance.

There are few schools who cannot muster flutes, clarinets and trumpets, but the larger instruments are expensive. If one has to choose, it is wise to plump for trombones next since these can cope with both tenor and bass parts and are also useful in orchestras and brass bands. Initially, bassoons are financially beyond the reach of many schools and have to be put aside until later. At this stage it is unavoidable that the ensemble is rather top-heavy. However, the four basic parts are covered:

	Division of parts
Soprano	flutes, clarinet I, trumpet or cornet I
Alto	clarinet II, trumpet or cornet II
Tenor	clarinet III, trombone I
Bass	trombone II

With a mixed ensemble, descant recorders and first violins would take the soprano line. (Descant recorders would, of course, sound an octave above the written note.) Second violins would take the alto line and violas and cellos the tenor and bass lines respectively. Elementary flautists may be given the oboe parts as these lie within the rudimentary

58

register of the flute. In addition to this the 'grounded' flautists could well help keep beginner oboists up to pitch.

In point of fact the line-up given looks more top-heavy than it actually sounds as greater numbers of woodwind players are needed to balance the brass. Ungainly as it appears, it is this kind of instrumentation which is found in many schools today. It is stressed that this is merely a starting point and not, by any stretch of the imagination, the ideal complement. Later, as interest grows and with a generous admixture of lower wind and brass, the band's full potential will begin to materialise, but for the moment it is important to make a start with the forces available. If, at the start, we bemoan the lack of enthusiasm, it is our own fault for, even with the instruments available in most schools, it is possible to give an inkling of what can be attained by a full-voiced band.

Sometimes, when trying to maintain a balanced ensemble, one needs considerable powers of persuasion to match an instrument with the child's personality and physical attributes – for example to encourage a potential tuba player or would-be bass clarinettist. In order to achieve a working balance, it is necessary to have some kind of guide in establishing ratios for instrumental lessons. Of course, circumstances will differ from school to school depending on staffing, the instrumental provision made by the local authority and the number of instruments provided by the pupils themselves. The following guide does assume eventual transfer of instruments. That is to say some clarinet players opting for bass clarinet, perhaps one flautist specialising on piccolo and so on.

Ratio guide for instrumental lessons

flutes	7	5	4	3
oboes	2	2	1	1
clarinets	12	9	7	5
bassoons	2	2	1	1
saxophones	4	4	3	2
cornets/trumpets	5	4	3	3
horns	4	4	2	1
trombones	3	3	3	2
euphoniums	2	1	1	1
tuba	2	1	1	1
double bass	1	1	1	1
percussion	3	2	2	2
Potential band of:	47	38	29	23

Once the potential players taste success, if only briefly, the desire to proceed will be greatly increased. A visit by one of the Forces' bands, or an established local school or music centre band could prove a vital incentive during this time.

Eventually a band of between twenty-three and thirty-eight players could probably be divided into the following line-up. The optional instruments have been marked with an asterisk for some schools will have difficulty providing all but the essential parts.

piccolo*	1
first flute	2+
second flute*	2+
first oboe	1
second oboe*	1
E flat clarinet*	1
first B flat clarinet	2+
second B flat clarinet	2+
third B flat clarinet	2+
alto clarinet*	1
bass clarinet*	1
first bassoon	1
second bassoon*	1
first alto saxophone	1
second alto saxophone*	1
tenor saxophone	1
baritone saxophone*	1
first cornet/trumpet	1+
second cornet/trumpet	1+
third cornet/trumpet	1+
first horn	1
second horn	1
third horn*	1
fourth horn*	1
first trombone	1
second trombone	1
bass trombone	1
euphonium	
(parts are marked 'baritone' in American publications)	1
tuba	1
double bass/bass guitar*	1
timpani*	1
percussion	2 (1*)

* optional   + usually more

Often there will be many more flutes, clarinets and trumpets and these can be incorporated on the proviso that the balance is maintained.

Few school band funds can stretch to purchasing a contrabass clarinet though such a magnificent instrument could well be a possibility with a music centre band. On the whole, music centres can work towards a full-voiced wind orchestra.

Most brass band instruments can be included but before going further it is necessary to try to clear some of the fog of misapprehension and bewilderment over nomenclature. What we call a 'tenor horn' (belonging to the saxhorn family and shaped like a small baritone or euphonium), the Americans term an 'alto horn'. Where alto horn parts are supplied these should, of course, be given to tenor horn players but in the main only French horn parts are included in the standard set so tenor horn players will need to transpose them up a tone. There is similar confusion of terminology over the use of the word 'baritone'. Americans mean euphonium when they say baritone and not the slighter brass band counterpart of the same name.

Flugel horn parts are more common in Continental publications but in any case pose few problems as they can be given to lower cornet players. If individual trumpet and cornet parts are issued, it is desirable that they are played on the appropriate instruments. Nowadays, however, the two instruments can be made to sound so similar that few would be able to differentiate. This last remark, although not calculated to goad cornet and trumpet players, will doubtless cause some of them to recoil in anger. We might appease them by conceding that given the trumpet's incisiveness and cornet's mellowness, both are capable of producing a legato and ensemble sound. Of course, when cornet and trumpet players play characteristically according to their instrument's distinctive qualities, a new dimension is added to the wind band. Alas, the luxury of having both players is not given to every band and the parts are necessarily substituted.

Judging by the considerable number of American publishers who still issue both treble and bass clef baritone parts, there must be almost as great a need for treble clef parts in the States as there is here, though for former trumpet players rather than brass band euphoniumists. Most modern scores include parts for C piccolo, the D flat piccolo being almost entirely discarded nowadays.

Having brought the band together we need to decide on some kind of seating plan. Without careful thought the band can be cobbled together in such a way that the most unlikely combinations of instruments end up cheek by jowl, the resultant sound being as muddled as it looks confused. Insomuch as positioning can increase awareness of tuning and balance it is important to establish a plan from the start. There are many conflicting ideas which have their own advantages and disadvantages, so all we can do is to keep certain practical criteria in mind.

Sections will play more in tune if they are separated from one another, and the positioning of sections should be determined by similarity of tone colour. For example horns and saxophones work well together while bassoons placed close to euphoniums become almost inaudible when in tune and all too audible when not – they are better widely separated. The following diagram suggests a seating arrangement. Wherever possible, principal players are placed together in the centre, as in the wind section of the modern symphony orchestra. The reasons for this are two-fold; firstly, grouping the more able players in the centre ensures a solid core which can lead the others and makes the band more controllable for the conductor; secondly, principal players are usually more able to iron out slight differences in intonation and to check phrasing and articulation if they can hear one another. This, however, is only one possibility and bands should experiment with other seating arrangements.

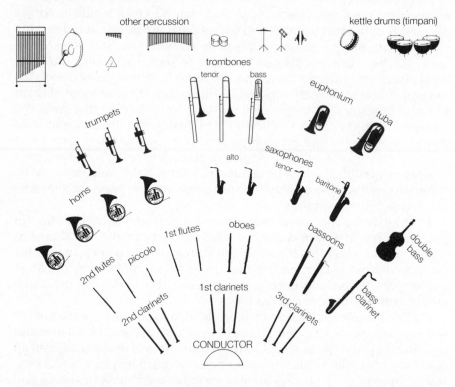

Flutes are seated on the conductor's left because the sound is produced on the player's right side and should be directed towards the audience. The same principle has been applied to the position of the French horns. The piccolo player (singular; two are a positive menace and would, in any case, be unlikely with beginner bands) will have little difficulty projecting and is best placed to the left of the conductor, next to the first flutes with whom he will need to tune octaves very carefully.

The backbone of the band is, of course, the clarinet section which should form a complete semicircle. Although there will be more clarinets than any other single type of instrument, they will need to be in the forefront as they carry much of the tune. Further, second and third parts are often written in the less-audible *chalumeau* register. Also, a certain unity of sound is achieved by having all the clarinets in a row.

The saxophones, really hybrids, are placed centrally and can blend with woodwind or brass or remain distinct. Often the horns have more in common with the woodwind tone than the brass and, again as in the orchestra, they are brought forward to project their sound. The traditional place of the percussion is at the very back, which allows freedom of movement to switch from one instrument to another quickly but, occasionally, with a lighter programme, there is much to be said for bringing the kit forward as in the dance band.

The same plan can be adapted to include strings and recorders for the junior school mixed ensemble. As the plan closely resembles the seating of the orchestral wind and brass sections, violins and cellos should, of course, take up their normal positions in front, violins to the conductor's left and cellos with the other basses to the right. Recorders are best placed with the flutes and oboes.

Many school stages are shallow and wide and therefore tend to spread the band rather too thinly, making it difficult for players at the extremes who either cannot hear the other side, or receive a distorted impression of balance and then adjust the dynamic of their playing accordingly. Movable blocks can be used to tier the band for maximum aural and visual effect. Again, a mat placed under the drums will prevent the blocks from acting as amplifiers although percussionists do tend to become disgruntled.

8 Rehearsals

Rehearsals for school band are usually included in a range of out-of-class activities and precluded from the timetable, although this is being challenged now by some schools. Often the rehearsals have, by necessity, to take place after school when players may be tired physically and mentally, and music centre bands have little choice but to rehearse out of class time. With this in mind, it is the teacher's task to ensure that, whilst working the band hard and obtaining as much as is musically possible, the rehearsal is both stimulating and enjoyable. The two goals are not at odds. By adopting an attitude of encouragement and co-operation, conductor-teachers can build a rapport with band members that will last long after those pupils have left school. Naturally, there are times when we have to chide a certain player for lack of practice, but this can be done tactfully and the point made that it is his or her playing that we object to, not the player personally.

If we accept an enthusiastic attitude as central to the activity, then to what extent can we attend to players' general musical education as a whole, rather than train them merely as bandsmen and bandswomen? Clearly, much depends on our notion of a general musical education and of a 'bandsperson', but the real issue here is one of process and product, or rather rehearsal and performance. The aims of the band in school and music centre are educative rather than performance-centred. Performance is not the ultimate goal but education by way of performance. It should be a natural outcome of rehearsal, thought of as part-and-parcel of a process instead of as the product.

Particularly during the summer months, the band may well have a busy concert schedule, requiring several varied programmes. Lasting all-round musicianship can hardly be instilled if we are constantly looking at short-term objectives, always working towards forthcoming public performances. Such practice makes a nonsense of the band and results not in music education, but merely 'instrumental operatives'. Not surprisingly with bands that are mechanically trained, we may detect a certain lack of intensity with expression markings and generally the music fails to come alive.

How then should the rehearsals be structured? The short answer to this must be 'long-term'. Players will then have the time to listen critically to themselves, to others, and thus to gel as a group. This approach has worked with considerable success in brass bands for years, helped no doubt by the homogeneity of the ensemble. In a sense the band forces the players to listen. The process is not one of osmosis but of comparison and, in turn, of change.

Time is always in short supply so it is vital to utilise the rehearsal period to its fullest extent. A rehearsal should have variety and be programme-planned. Many rehearsals appear to grind to a halt because of a lack of direction. There is much to be said for starting with a warm-up: something short and well within the technical capabilities of the band. Published warm-up studies – including long notes, arpeggios and rhythm patterns – are available. Apart from warming-up the instrument and assisting players to 'set' their embouchures, it provides impetus and motivation, as well as a springboard to other, more serious music.

To keep the interest alive during an intensive rehearsal, it is valuable to change course or direction either by a change of styles or by choosing a work in which the emphasis is on different players. Not only do those playing inside parts need some of the limelight from time to time but they should also be aware of their contribution to the totality of the sound. Further to this, it is unwise to spend too long on individual players and sections when they can be rehearsed separately at a later stage, preventing the other players from becoming impatient. Similarly, players will become bored if too much time is spent on one work, especially if concentrating on technical aspects. It is unprofitable to repeat large sections of the music without telling the band why. Except for those who happen to have lost their place, players find it disturbing if they continually start and stop. It is, then, important to preserve the continuity of the rehearsal.

A portion of regular rehearsal time should be preserved for sight reading and new music, some of which may never reach the standard required for a public performance. Providing new stimulus is essential if the band is to remain a developing entity. Clearly some of the sight reading will be chosen to improve certain technical difficulties, but occasionally we should deliberately select a work which though ostensibly straightforward, requires great expressiveness. In this way the players come to know something of the interpretative qualities which are required and they should begin to play more sensitively. It is a loss of objectives when kindred technical skills are acquired at the expense of aesthetic responsiveness and a genuine love of music. Surely the whole point is to develop musicianship, aural awareness and sensitivity of feeling.

By far the most fruitful method of taking a band through a new work is to play straight through the piece, unless, of course, there is a total breakdown, in which case the music should be taken from a suitable point rather than restarted. It is one of the traditional maxims of teaching that we begin with a conceptual understanding of the whole, then, and only then, proceed to a detailed knowledge of its constituent parts. In giving the players an overall impression of the music we help the sight reading process but, more importantly, the piece itself becomes more meaningful. Similarly, by explaining why we want the clarinets to play softly here, or a flute passage brought out there, by relating melody to accompaniment, foreground to background and colour to texture, instead of merely issuing unenlightening directives, 'do this, do that,' eventually the players will begin to view their part within the overall scheme of the work. Inasmuch as one is emphasising positive musical (as opposed to technical) details, the players see their parts as having more import, and they respond accordingly.

Shifting to actuality, we might now tease out some of the problems which constantly crop up in wind band rehearsals and look for ways of solving them.

Rehearsal points

Probably the most common problem is that of clarinet squeaks. This appears to be contagious and the sooner it is remedied the better for all concerned. Often squeaking can be caused by a reed which is damaged in some way (perhaps warped or uneven), by placing too much of the mouthpiece in the mouth, or simply by blowing too hard.

Precision of attack, especially at the start of a piece, is a rare quality and 'split' notes, as they are colloquially known, seem particularly prevalent with trumpet and horn players. It should be made clear to them that to start a note involves the tongue withdrawing not striking. Apart from placing the tongue correctly (behind the front top teeth) the syllable may be too forced; 'Du' is preferable to 'Tu' especially in the higher register where the harmonics are closer together. Obviously the syllable used will need to be altered depending on whether a particular passage is marcato or legato.

The breathy sound produced by inexperienced flautists is frequently caused by the aperture of the lips being too great. Often this can be eliminated by reducing the size of the aperture compressing the air, coupled with a more gentle blowing action.

Often we hear school bands 'pecking' notes in an attempt to achieve fast staccato playing. There is an illusion here: the tongue and throat muscles are kept relaxed and the notes slightly lengthened (rather than shortened) yet kept up to pace, thus producing notes which speak more clearly, and an eloquent staccato. It should be explained that staccato is better thought of as a lightness rather than a shortness.

Wind bands are notorious for playing too loudly. Dynamics, balance and blend are relative to the acoustical quality of the setting, and style and character of the music.

Phrasing is too often ignored on the pretext of inadequate breath control. Save for the larger instruments, the flutes, oboes, clarinets and trumpets should be able to sustain (as an exercise, never in performance) a hymn-tune from start to finish, without breathing in the middle.

Military bands are renowned for their sense of discipline and posture. Unfortunately, we see many school bands whose members sit in a slovenly and incorrect fashion, the result sounding as bad as it looks. Bad habits formed when young are difficult to correct in later years and can lead to embouchure and breathing problems. Deportment is essential for confident, reliable playing, as well as the general demeanour of the band. A guarded note has to be struck here: the deportment of the military bands is to be admired but emulated only on the proviso that it is not at the expense of the music.

Tuning

Wind bands, by their very nature, are more difficult to tune than brass bands, in which the instruments are closely related. A renowned band adjudicator once remarked that he would rather tune a dozen brass bands than one military band. In school bands the problems are intensified with beginner oboists and almost self-taught saxophonists. There have been many theories on wind band tuning but no hard and fast rules can be laid down. It is largely a matter of compromise. The main ingredients of good tuning, in woodwind or brass, are attentive listening and a well-formed, flexible embouchure, without which the ultimate result can never be wholly satisfactory however many tuning notes are deployed.

Using more than one tuning note has been favoured in recent years, for example, concert A for flutes and oboes, F for trumpets and clarinets sounding a major third. Unfortunately, to use these notes with the lower brass and wind would create 'resultant' tones – a growling effect caused by close harmony placed low in the band. Whilst the idea seems to work well for the upper instruments and even French horns, the E flat instruments have a choice of playing either D or F sharp (sounding F and A respectively) neither of which are open harmonic series notes.

The chord of B flat, a traditional brass band tuning chord, has many advantages. Using F for second trumpets, third clarinets and French horns, and B flat for the B flat and E flat instruments (written C and G respectively), means that the majority of instruments play either their pitch notes or open harmonic series notes. It is the C instruments at a disadvantage this time. B flat or F would be appropriate, then separately unison Cs, taking the B flat as a source of reference – as in an ascending major scale. Once satisfactory, building the sections up chordally to produce a resounding chord of B flat can be used as a final check.

The general level of intonation will, of course, vary according to a whole variety of factors: the key of the music; the seating arrangement; the endurance of the players; the availability of good instruments and mouthpieces; the temperature and humidity; the players' ability to keep their instruments warm; the tonal balance; and the degree of compromise of certain acknowledged suspect notes – for instance, the fourth partial (middle E, E flat and D on the trumpet) is slightly flat, although this can be compensated for by players with a sensitive ear and flexible lip position. A properly structured rehearsal, giving each section sufficient non-playing time, will ensure that the tuning remains true to the end. Similarly, sensible programme planning will help endurance and in turn the general level of intonation, and careful positioning of the players can greatly increase tuning awareness.

Occasionally, what at first seems to be poor intonation, is simply a lack of tonal balance. Overblown clarinets or underblown larger instruments can create an imbalance that is particularly noticeable in chordal and cadential passages, particularly if the third of the chord is being underplayed. The key of the music can also have an adverse effect on intonation. Even when the temperature and humidity are satisfactory, players who are resting must ensure that their instruments are kept warm by gently blowing through them. This is one of the most common causes of poor intonation, particularly with piccolo and brass players. It should be added that the tuning of the whole band ought not to be at the very outset of the rehearsal, but perhaps after the first piece when the instruments are warm.

9 Writing for wind band

This is hardly the place to talk of wind band scoring *per se* – besides, there are already several adequate books available which are devoted entirely to this study. The present chapter is concerned with the practical considerations which need to be taken into account when writing, (either arranging or composing) for the average music centre or oddly-assorted school band. It is heartening for the rest of us to know that, when arranging for wind band, Mendelssohn occasionally got it wrong, and Haydn is reputed to have said, 'I have only just learned in my old age how to use wind instruments.'

Home-spun compositions and arrangements have many advantages provided that they are well-tailored. By writing with a particular band in mind, both beginners and advanced players can be stretched, and balance problems and peculiarities in instrumentation can, to some extent, be made more acceptable. Of course, the technical limitations will often impose certain scoring restrictions but, by the same token, they may well prompt us to formulate more imaginative parts. This does, however, place considerable emphasis on our skill as arrangers and in many ways it is easier to write for advanced players, but as Kodály pointed out, 'Nobody should be above writing for children: on the contrary, we should strive to become good enough to do so.'

Naturally, parts which are technically demanding are assigned to the more advanced players. At the other extreme, those who have reached only an elementary standard of achievement are given specially designed 'filler' parts. As the players develop, new pieces can be scored to suit their capabilities, thus ensuring optimum rate of progress. For the teacher-arranger there is yet another advantage, namely, that by writing for instrumentalists of a variety of standards, we gain a practical knowledge of instrumentation the like of which cannot be gleaned from the pages of orchestration textbooks. Moreover, such commonsense know-how is invaluable in rehearsal.

The scope of the music possible will depend, to some degree, on the instrumental resources available. Compositionally, we should think in terms of the sounds and capabilities of the instruments to spark off the

69

imaginative processes rather than transcribing, as an afterthought, something wrought at the piano. With arrangements, it is important to choose works which lend themselves to wind and brass treatment. Moreover, we should consider whether an intended transcription would be tasteful as well as feasible. Some of the published arrangements would set the teeth on edge of those with catholic tastes, let alone the musical purists.

It is misleading to talk of an 'arrangement' when what is really meant is a 'transcription'. This confusion arises partly from misuse, and partly from those who have a vested interest in preserving the term 'arrangement' intact and so claiming more than is due to them. What counts as an arrangement is determined by a degree of originality, whilst 'transcription' has a more circumscribed connotation, implying a straightforward transference of material to the band medium. We might regard a nineteenth-century orchestral overture as a transcription whereas an original setting of a folk song would qualify as an arrangement. Of course, it is not always quite so easy to differentiate between transcriptions and arrangements.

With music in a pop idiom, an imaginative approach by the arranger is preferable, that is taking an original melody line and reworking the harmonies and accompaniment in the band medium, rather than a mere transcription of the original. In any case, popular piano reductions are often simplified to the extent that essential notes are missing, the voicings may be so low as to 'grumble', and it is not unusual to find totally incorrect chords. One published version of a song appears as:

whilst another:

The example has been transposed for ease of comparison. There are times, however, when subtle chord substitution can lift a song to make it appear almost magical. This is taken from the same song:

Rhythmic ostinato bass lines work well and have instant appeal to euphoniumists and tuba players who complain of 'never having a tune'. 'Scarborough Fair' (Hal Leonard), is a particularly effective example and although more folk than pop, it has been given an up-tempo accompaniment.

With lighter music, it is far better to sound well in the band idiom rather than try to recreate the original sounds. But with a more serious work, the transcription must follow with the stream of the composer's intention and catch the likeness of the original sounds if the work is to be at all plausible. If the work is incongruous to the band's mode of expression, then a transcription has little purpose. Moreover, the transcriber would be abrogating his or her responsibility both to the composer and to the original composition.

Primarily, the pieces for the less-experienced players will be rhythmically uncomplicated, have little independence of movement, and will be placed within the elementary middle range. Rhythmically, it is as well to have only one part syncopated at a time. The following example is something of a compromise. The chord* was delayed slightly to help co-ordinate the bass and inside parts. The second example gives the original rhythm.

Pitchwise, it is difficult at the beginner stage to strike a balance between simplicity and boredom. Nevertheless, by utilising all the technique the players can muster (and five notes may well be their ceiling) the parts become more interesting and have greater meaning. Little musicianship is gained from playing one note albeit at the right pitch and at the right time. In this respect, the nineteenth-century Russian horn bands, in which each player was allocated only one note, pushed absurdity to the limit. Undoubtedly there is much that can be done using only one note, depending on the way in which it is used. *One Note Samba,* a marvellously economic piece, contains rather more than one note despite its title. Furthermore, the reiteration of the one note is of secondary importance, the interest being primarily rhythmic and harmonic.

The personnel of a school and music centre band may change year by year. Although the teacher will know the present forces of the band he or she is writing for, if the arrangement is to be of use in the future, the scoring should be designed so that certain essential parts can easily be covered. Scoring is a time-consuming job without having to re-arrange the same piece several times. To obtain maximum mileage from one score, it is advisable to cue-in essential parts; cross-scoring can sound thick and bland. By adopting the following scheme, it is possible to achieve, in one arrangement, a degree of flexibility. It ensures that the overall result is reasonably complete when played by a small ensemble, without sounding overladen and congested played by the full complement.

Initially, the scoring is restricted to eight essential parts, using the instruments most schools can readily obtain. All the other parts are optional. The essential parts are: flute; clarinets 1, 2 and 3; trumpets 1 and 2; trombones; and one bass part played either by another trombone, double (string) bass, or E flat tuba. Other parts may carry important material from time to time, but this would be cued in the essential parts as well. Having made the distinction between essential and optional parts, it is necessary to add that some are more optional than others. Saxophones (altos 1, 2, and tenor) and euphonium are present often enough to justify having their own parts. Although these are not essential they can be described as highly desirable since, by and large, they will add countermelodies and greater interest. Similarly, it should also be noted that although in the scheme as outlined, there are only two essential trombone parts, it is more usual to write for three trombones. This enables the arranger to write triads for the complete section. Moreover, if a tuba player is present, but there are only two trombonists, the player formerly reading the third part can transfer to second trombone thus giving the impression of a complete trombone section and avoiding a doubled bass line. The practical implications of the scheme can be seen more clearly in the piece on page 74. The essential parts are marked with an asterisk.

Some authorities suggest starting by scoring a hymn tune. The reason for this may lie in the belief that hymns are relatively straightforward. Unfortunately, being chordal, they are apt to highlight slight differences in intonation, in much the same way that unisons do. Whilst at a later stage this may be desirable in rehearsal, it is hardly likely to inspire confidence from new recruits. Moreover, although hymns are stock-in-trade for the organist, when played by the wind band they are not particularly effective and have little in common with other types of music the band is likely to encounter. The players might just as well become accustomed to playing rhythmically independent parts from the start, however simple. After all, this is one of the main advantages of ensemble work. A chorale played by the brass, or even by four clarinets, can sound stunning but it needs experienced players to do it justice.

Folk songs and late sixteenth- and early seventeenth-century Venetian antiphonal music are especially suited to variable instrumentation. In antiphonal music the separate instrumental choirs can be made up with whatever instruments are to hand, but primary colours – woodwind against brass – make a striking contrast. Venetian spatial and antiphonal effects are equally impressive today. The example on pages 76–7 is taken from *Flourish for Wind Band* by Vaughan Williams.

Continental sources reveal traditional folk melodies and aubades played by waits on official occasions. *Marche de la Procession Dansante* (see pages 78–9) is performed each year at Echternach on the Tuesday of Pentecost.

Nowadays, complete fingering charts can be purchased. These are

from Intrada (originally tower music) by Pezel

arr. K. Thompson

Tambour or S.D. without snare

printed on card and can be used in a loose-leaf format. They are invaluable not only for the non-specialist avoiding awkward fingering patterns in an arrangement, but also for assisting beginners in rehearsal.

Whilst not advocating that arrangers indicate fingering patterns, there are times when suggesting an alternative fingering can make clear something which could be potentially confusing. For instance, here it was better to write in 'trill with thumb' than leave an elementary flautist guessing:

With beginner pieces, second and third clarinet parts are usually kept below the break, but, more importantly, it is wise to avoid writing rapid passages across the throat and clarino registers:

To help intonation, high notes should be divided, marked 'divisi' and the higher of the two given to players with secure top registers. This is particularly important with the two oboe and alto saxophone parts:

Alternatively, a simplified passage marked 'ossia' can be given. It is more usual to include the latter under the difficult section:

With beginner pieces, second and third clarinet parts are usually kept below the break, but, more importantly, it is wise to avoid writing rapid passages across the throat and clarino registers:

Trombone slide positions need to be considered to avoid ungainly and 'alcoholic' glissandi. Occasionally this facility can be exploited provided that the work lends itself to this kind of burlesque treatment. The effect does, however, pall with over-use.

Flourish for Wind Band

R. Vaughan Williams

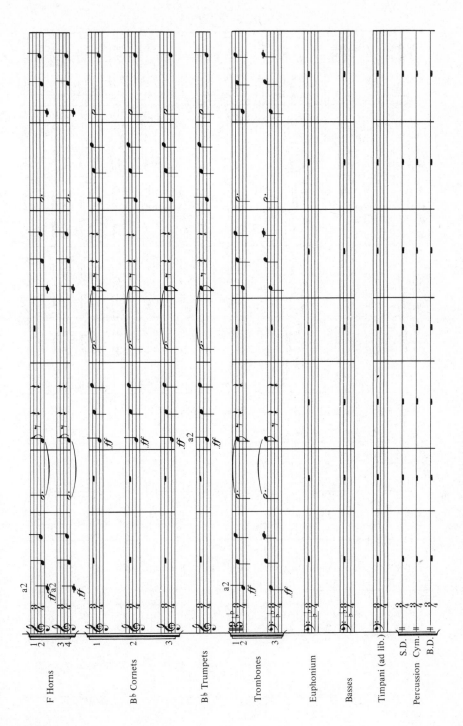

Marche de la Procession Dansante

arr. K. Thompson

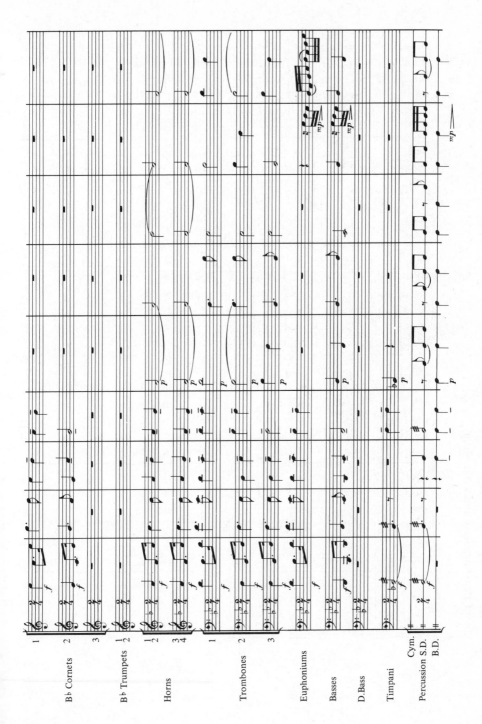

from Proclamation and Folk Song

Kevin Thompson

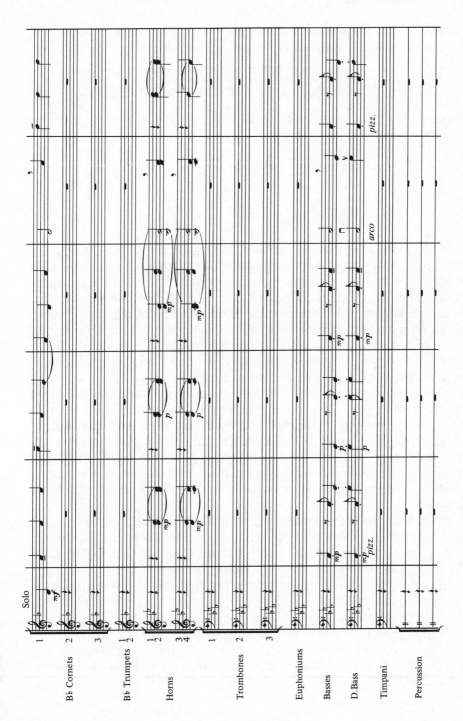

81

One way of simplifying a demanding rapid passage is to divide the part, making sure to 'dovetail', so that it flows naturally:

Similarly, long sustained passages can be made easier by staggering the breathing, on the proviso that there are several players to a part:

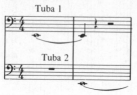

When writing for the kit drummer, the part will usually be taken as a guide only. It is worth remembering that used without the snare the side drum can be made to sound medieval and tambour-like. Orchestral percussion (usually two players) will require more detailed writing. On the whole, these percussionists are more dexterous when it comes to playing a roll, flam, or ruff, but they may find it difficult to 'swing', unlike the kit drummers. Nowadays when writing for timpani, it is usual to indicate flats and sharps against the corresponding notes rather than merely to state the required key in the margin as before.

The rôle of the double bass or bass guitar is two-fold, harmonic and rhythmic. In a soft, slow moving passage it can provide a subtle bass line, yet one which adds impetus. With pop numbers, imaginative players will often busy the basic part and, as with an experienced drummer, they can extemporise a far better part than could be written. Naturally, much will depend for whom the part is written. In some cases all that is required is to map out the basic structure and include chord symbols.

Because of the greater dynamic strength of the brass, there is a tendency for it to cover much of the woodwind detail, especially the flute part. Legato cornet or trumpet melodies set against contrasting rhythmic and melodic figures work well (see pages 80–1).

In general, the wind band prefers flat keys, the majority of instruments being B flat and E flat. The simplest keys are probably F and B flat, as these put the B flat instruments into G and C respectively. It does, however, become monotonous if one is restricted to a small cycle of keys. As the band develops, the range of tonality should gradually widen. Sometimes, in a long concert, or rehearsal, a remote key can be balm on the ear.

10   Music for wind band

It is a widely held view that a substantial proportion of the repertoire for wind band is musically artless. Far from attempting to prove otherwise, for the writer willingly concedes the shortcomings of much of the music that has come to form the staple fare of school and music centre bands, the present chapter is intended to show something of the scope of the music generally. Furthermore, the chapter deals with recently composed music for band, and suggests replacing overexposed works with some that really ought to see the light of day again.

From the start, suitable sources of music have to be actively sought. Much of the early repertoire is, at best, transient. This is regrettable as beginner bands often work on two or three pieces for a whole term and some of the pieces become irksome after only a few rehearsals. Apropos of this, there is a lot to be said for following one of the published band courses, provided that we take the trouble to dip into other pieces. Several of the American courses come complete with cassettes and these can be used for practice by groups or individuals. Another advantage with the complete 'package', is that many of the pieces are short and repetitive yet long enough to be of musical value.

As well as choosing music which is worthwhile in terms of musical content, it is important to involve everyone. This not only unites the band but also helps the overall sound. Experience has shown that in the initial stages there is safety in numbers. Quite apart from evening-out slight differences in intonation, players become more confident *en masse*.

Music for beginner band

Often the problem in choosing music for beginner band is one of having the right number of parts: usually there are either too few or too many. Works intended for military band are surprisingly small scale and, in any case, are too advanced at this stage. Conversely, those pieces scored for American High School bands of gargantuan proportions are also impractical unless the essential parts are indicated. Thankfully, a number of publishers on both sides of the Atlantic are realising the needs of beginner bands by issuing pieces which either require the minimum of technique, or are arranged in such a way that, providing there is a quorum of players, they sound complete. These functional or utility arrangements are particularly apt at the outset and it is for this reason that considerable space has been given here to discussing them. Starting with mixed ensemble scores and continuing through to arrangements especially intended for wind band, the suggestions are proffered as a guide and do not represent the only way of setting out.

Although not specifically intended for wind band, 'Music Kit Series' (Middle Eight) – comprising *Music Kit, Classical Music Kit* and *Christmas Carol Kit* – is designed to cater for almost any combination of players and is readily adaptable as parts are included for C, B flat and F instruments. The format and approach are similar in each of the three series. In all cases the instrumentation is extremely flexible and, with the exception of the bass part, enough parts are provided to cater for most beginner bands. It should be pointed out, however, that as these arrangements are designed with elementary string players in mind, generally the keys are more suited to those instruments. The piano part can be dispensed with provided most of the parts are covered. The minimum combination is one player (on C, or B flat melody) plus piano.

Fun Music Ensemble (Chappell), arranged by B. Turner, is analogous to the music kit idea in that it is scored for almost any combination of instruments. Each instrument part contains a harmonic 'band' part, a melodic line and, with the exception of the guitar part, a piano accompaniment. This allows for solos, duets, trios, quartets, right up to full ensemble. As is to be expected from such comprehensive, overladen scoring, with a full-voiced ensemble the arrangements can hardly be very subtle and, to be fair, they are not intended to be. All six titles are culled from the pop tunes of yesterday or the day before. An extension of the above and comparable to *Classical Music Kit*, is *Fun Music Classics* (Chappell), a pot-pourri of semi-classics which includes Purcell's *Rondo from Abdelazer* (issued recently by three separate publishers in various forms).

Windscores, arranged by Lawton (Novello), though not intended for beginners, may be especially useful to schools with established orchestras which need to make more of their brass and woodwind players, whilst at the same time retaining the strings. The scoring is such that the wind parts can be used independently of the strings, but by far the most useful aspect with this type of arrangement is that cellos and basses can be employed if, as is often the case, there is a lack of lower wind and brass players. The aim of the series is, according to the publisher's blurb, 'to provide for all likely combinations of instruments found in schools and amateur societies in this age of wind'. The initial five pieces from a total of twelve are restricted to SATB harmonisation and, provided that the basic parts are covered, are feasible with small bands. The choice of material is refined and the arrangements well-crafted. On a par to *Windscores*, *Band/Orchestra Concert Folio*, arranged by Gordon (Chappell), is a collection of seven easy pieces playable by wind, strings or almost any combination of wind band instruments.

Atarah's Band Kits (Novello), provide a bridge from classroom to bandroom. The units B1, *Getting it Together*, and C1, *The Elastic Band*, have nicely bicultural, appealing pieces from classics to tin pan alley. Flexibly arranged by John Harper for virtually any combination of instruments, it even provides for guitars and synthesizer.

The 'Contemporary Band Course' (Belwin Mills) is a systematic and comprehensive graded band method. The basic books, called *Band Today*, catering for individual, group and especially full-band tuition, are invaluable for group lessons. The explanations are lucid; the format attractive to children. Correlated to the basic tutor books, are supplementary studies, ensemble material, individual arrangements and instrumental solos. *Band Sembles*, part of the ensemble material, is, as the newly-coined title suggests, playable by either ensemble or full band. Scored in basic SATB, each book contains all four parts. This allows woodwind and brass to play separately, to be divided or mixed as required. The individual arrangements and the 'Band Encounter' series are particularly rewarding. Belwin Mills also publish the second minuet from the *Royal Fireworks Music* by Handel, in a very easy arrangement by Acton Ostling (not to be confused with Eric Osterling, another American band arranger). Luverne, amongst others, publish music specifically aimed at the junior band but, unfortunately, many of these elementary pieces have titles which make us flinch, and therefore we avoid them.

Put Them Together (Reakes), Stuart Johnson's initial departure from brass to wind band, sets out to provide 'easy music, suitable for concert use, for the growing number of wind and brass instrumentalists in schools and music centres'. A more recent tutor, *The First Stuart Johnson Wind Band Book* (R. Smith), is also serviceable as the pieces are playable by small wind groups up to full wind band. The pieces range from classics to folk music and include an original composition. The optional parts for brass band instruments are especially useful. Not to be confused with *Put Them Together* is *Play Them Together*, arranged by Waddington (Piper Publications), a collection of eleven rounds for almost any group of instruments.

Of particular interest for those of us who in the past have been lumbered with surplus copies is *A Second Wind Band Book*, edited and arranged by Bram Wiggins (OUP), because the twenty-nine parts, eleven of which are optional, may be purchased separately. Further-more, parts are available for treble clef euphonium and E flat bass. The pieces are both well chosen and tastefully scored. There is an optional posthorn part in the Mozart *Sleigh Ride*.

Chester Music came in with a late but timely run. Its series sports the name of 'Bandstand', and comprises two albums for junior band. Again edited by Bram Wiggins, who also offers helpful introductory advice, the albums are a compilation of warm-ups, scales, arrangements and compositions with salad days appeal. Both albums come complete with piano reductions and are cross-cued for incomplete ensembles. Book one comprises seasoned folksongs, original miniatures, classical and bucolic dances. Book two, technically tougher and stronger in express-ive fibre, has representatives both from home (Berkeley and Burgon) and from France (Franck, Satie, and Auric, whose endearing, bitter-sweet *Song from the Moulin Rouge* is redolent of Montmartre), alongside more familiar material. The series has been durably packaged if hurriedly proof-read.

In the past, one of the offshoots of the American publishers' near monopoly of elementary band music, was countless arrangements of national songs, hymns and Christmas carols, the settings of which were totally unknown to British children. John Kinyon, a name engrained on the minds of many young wind players, is almost single-handedly responsible for a large number of these arrangements. Despite the parochial nature of the settings, he has the knack of writing parts which are both comfortably placed and rhythmically uncomplicated. His 'Mini-Score' series (Alfred Music) is apparently designed for incom-plete bands yet the essential parts (and there have to be some) are not indicated. Probably more useful at this stage is *The MPH John Kinyon Band Method* (Chappell), specifically designed for 'beginner band or classes of instruments'.

A considerable number of publishers are marketing easy, small wind ensemble music and purely woodwind groups will find the following publications of use: *Chalumeau Canons* by John Robert Brown (Chappell), a book of low register canons designed for elementary clarinettists and progressively arranged in order of difficulty; *Six Pieces for Woodwind Groups* arranged by Carter, (OUP), containing tastefully-chosen pieces arranged for two flutes, two oboes, four clarinets and bassoon, though clarinet four and bassoon have the bass part (sometimes an octave apart) making one of the two dispensable; *Options for Woodwind*, edited by Alan Cave (Middle Eight), compris-ing four main parts transposed for either B flat or C instruments – French horn players may also be included; *Mixed Bag* edited by Graham

Lyons, scored for a range of abilities acknowledging that players develop at different rates (extra elementary parts are also included); and *Workbook for Woodwind* by Philippe Oboussier (Novello) which is an elementary group method with useful detachable fingering charts for the non-specialist.

'Pre-Red Band' series (Pro Art Publications) is simplicity itself. Prior to, and derived from each piece, there are scale, chord and rhythm studies ensuring that the band starts off in key, in time and in tune – a useful exercise. The sequel, for those who have graduated from the previous pieces, is the 'Red Band' series, a selection of titles generally well-scored and selected, though the choice of the C.P.E. Bach *Solfeggio* is ill-fitting, the arrangement gauche and hard to reconcile.

There are also some useful arrangements from the classics. Brahms' *The Hungarian Dance No. 5*, arranged by Sebesky, is part of the Studio series for elementary bands, which includes a piano part for rehearsal purposes (perhaps a mixed blessing). Parts are written within a limited range, but the key could have been better chosen because C instruments are required to play in F minor. Purcell's *Song of Victory from King Arthur*, arranged by Gordon (Bourne), has both short and full scores. Ideal for elementary bands, there is thoughtful *divisi* in the higher cornet parts. *The Norse Song* by Schumann, arranged by Gordon (Edward Marks Music Corp.), is an arrangement of *Nordisches Lied* from *Album for the Young*. It is of approximately grade 3 to 4 standard. Only the condensed score is available.

Music for intermediate band

For bands beyond the beginner and elementary stages, 'The Growing Band Series' (Alfred Music), provides music up to an intermediate level. *Triumphant Festival from Music for the Royal Fireworks* by Handel, arranged by Kinyon, is a particularly well-scored example, despite the erroneous title which should read *La Rejouissance from the Royal Fireworks Music*. Also in the same series is *Finale Grandioso* from the opera *Julius Caesar*, arranged by Gordon. Performance notes are included and again Gordon writes optional high notes for clarinets.

The present writer's own tutor . . . *And The Band Played On* (R. Smith), aims to provide a range of music for both the complete music centre complement and the kind of instrumental resources available in most schools; parts for brass band players are provided.

Flourish for Wind Band by Vaughan Williams (OUP) is a beautifully scored, concise piece. Ostensibly straightforward, it requires great expressiveness. Characterised by its subtle tone colour changes, antiphonal effects, modal melodies and parallel motion, it is in true Vaughan Williams' style (see pages 76–7).

Highlights from Jesus Christ Superstar by Andrew Lloyd Webber, arranged by O'Brien (Leeds Music Corp.), is a well-placed arrangement, again intended for the young concert band and is impressive and rather 'big-band' in style. Suitable for an end-of-term concert, the selection is exceedingly popular with secondary school children.

Clare Grundman's *Little Suite for Band* (Boosey & Hawkes) needs a sensitive cornet player for the subtle muted solo in the second movement. Band parts are of approximately grade 5 standard. Bands of this ability would find *March* from Symphony No. 2 by Tchaikovsky, arranged by Gordon (Marks Music Corp.), *Capriccio Italien* by Tchaikovsky, arranged by Cacavas (Luverne), and *A Night at the Ballet* arranged by Walters (Rubank), well within their grasp. The American trumpeter, Robert Nagel, has arranged a *Baroque Trumpet Suite* (Marks Music Corp.) from works by Handel originally for trumpet, oboes and strings. If we must play, yet again, *The Grand March* from *Aïda* the arrangement by Eymann (Belwin Mills) is as worthy as most.

If the impression has been given of there being a glut of pieces strung together in series, then it is to understate the obvious. Belwin Mills publish a 'Band and Record' series, along with many other American publishing houses, in which demonstration discs are provided; R. Smith and Jenson (USA) market their joint publications by first forwarding give-away sampler albums; but to cap them all, there is actually an 'Elastic Band' series – presumably intended to stretch the band. In this series comes Richard Rodney Bennett's beautiful and haunting *Theme from Nicholas and Alexandra* arranged by Bullock (Colgems Music Corp.): a delicate but perhaps too sparse arrangement.

Traditionally, military band marches are published without full scores, so conductors have to make the best of a heavily cued solo cornet part. The marches of Kenneth Alford (the British Sousa) are standard band fare and worthy technique builders. Much of the American marching band repertoire is intended for oversized and undernourished ensembles. It is technically awkward and of doubtful popularity.

The adroitness of Leroy Anderson never ceases to amaze, even if much of his music is now somewhat hackneyed and *passé*. Particularly effective is his *Christmas Festival* (Belwin Mills), a sparkling miscellany of ingeniously interwoven seasonal tunes, but the parts lie high.

There is certainly no shortage of lollipops for band; more imaginative than most is the programmatic *Morning Commuter* by Charles Spinney (Belwin Mills).

Suite Fantasque by Willy Hautvast (Molenaar) is written in a tongue-in-cheek, burlesque vein, and is a useful addition to the band repertoire not least because of its unusual scoring scheme. Even a cursory glance at the parts (for only a three-line condensed score is available) reveals more cross-scoring and doubling than usual. Indeed this international set – standard issue from the publisher – is designed so that the work is playable by brass bands, wind bands and the types of continental bands in which the most peculiar transposition takes place. Jibes of setting out for Utopia and ending up in Blunderland are easy, but rather than chaffing under the limits imposed, the scheme actually works and is safe, as much as utility scoring can be. However, with just a short score, and there's the rub, nobody knows where the interest lies. By far the most intriguing movement is *Danse Ternaire*, its essential cleverness being in the irregular metre.

Kendor Music (USA) publish many cleverly-arranged pieces of a lighter nature and possibly more appealing to their home market. Notable exceptions are *Polaris* by Fote, which is an easy concert march; and *Three Etchings* by Nestico – it has difficult first and third movements, full of energy and rhythmic drive, but an easier, closely-harmonised second movement with flute and woodwind solos over muted bell-tone effects in the brass.

Organ pieces can sound impressive scored for band. After all, the organ is essentially a wind instrument. There are many published arrangements of Bach fugues. These, by their very nature, that is their absolute independence of parts, transcribe particularly well for wind band. Mendelssohn's Fugue no. 3 in C minor (op. 37) has been arranged by Cacavas (Alfred Music), and is possible with the average school band.

Old Hundredth in the setting by Vaughan Williams, arranged by Washburn (OUP), can be used with string players by combining the arrangement with that of David Stone in the Oxford Amateur Orchestra Series. Complete with the famous brass fanfare opening, the arrangement is for unison, or mixed (SATB) choir, organ and band. Other music for performance in church could include *O How Amiable* by Vaughan Williams, adapted by Rosenthal, again for SATB and *Prelude on Brother James's Air* by Searle Wright, arranged by Young, based on the Gordon Jacob arrangement (both published by OUP).

Marches other than those cast in the traditional military band mould, could include: *Trojan March* by Berlioz (two versions, one published by Brons; another by Boston); *Marche Heroique* by Saint-Saëns, arranged by Winterbottom; *Alla Marcia* from the *Karelia Suite* by Sibelius, arranged by Richardson; and *The Earle of Oxford's March* from the *William Byrd Suite*, transcribed by Jacob (all published by Boosey and Hawkes).

Like the music of Vaughan Williams, much of Walton's music has been arranged for band: *Fanfare and Scotch Rhapsody*, amongst other dances from *Façade*, arranged by O'Brien (OUP); *Spitfire Fugue*, arranged by Wallace; and *Prelude to Richard III*, arranged by Richardson (both Boosey and Hawkes), not to mention a certain ceremonious march which crops up more than occasionally.

Fanfare and Soliloquy by Trevor Sharpe (Chappell), and *Trumpet Prelude* by Charpentier, arranged by Kenny (Herald Music), make a sparkling start to a concert. The latter, however, lies very high and is successful only with outstanding brass players.

Though originally published for brass band, *Concert Prelude* by Philip Sparke (R. Smith), might just as easily have been conceived for winds; imaginative scoring and full use of the tonal palette combine to produce a work well-wrought in wind band terms.

A Renaissance Suite is a collection of pieces by Melchior Frank, John Dowland and Thomas Morley, arranged by Whitney from the 'Insights into Music Series' (Alfred Music). Each part includes a lengthy yet excellent description of the musical period and the compositional techniques employed. These tasteful arrangements require full-voiced woodwind and brass sections as they split the band into separate instrumental choirs.

Music for advanced band

As is to be expected, bands of an advanced standard have a greater choice of music and it is easier to arrive at a suitable and balanced programme. Selections, light overtures and transcriptions are still trotted out with fair regularity but, searching through publishers' lists, it becomes increasingly obvious that the repertoire is more comprehensive than is at first apparent. In the past, orchestral transcriptions have served to confer symphonic status (perhaps in the vain hope that some of the social cachet would rub off) and occasional original works were inserted to lend an air of authenticity to a programme. Transcriptions of nineteenth-century overtures, many of which have become standards, are too numerous to cite. Without attempting to bolster or defend the trivia of much of the repertoire, there are some works still largely unnoticed. Inevitably, the main problem is one of selectivity. There are representative works from most of the musical periods as well as unhackneyed pieces by Copland, Grainger, Hindemith, Holst, Shostakovitch, Vaughan Williams and, more recently, Gordon Jacob and Stephen Dodgson who have each shown a remarkable interest in writing for wind band.

It is possible to find material which concurs with the recent trends in the classroom. There are early music pieces, folk songs, plausible Afro-

American numbers, and even graphic scores in simplified rhythmic form, though to link the wind band (as distinct from wind ensemble) with the avant-garde would be tenuous to say the least. Hitherto, wind bands have had a reputation for entertaining their audiences with sentimental nostalgia rather than introducing them to contemporary music. They have attracted the less radical, even distinctly retrospective composers, rather than the avant-gardists, despite encouraging moves in the brass band world.

There is a small but growing body of discerning people – conductors, performers and publishers – who are well-versed in the available literature and eager to promote British wind music. The wind band is not an ensemble somehow deracinated, torn from one culture and transplanted into another, but it is indigenous. It has not only survived, but of late, its popularity has burgeoned in schools and music centres. Doubtlessly, it is the repertoire of many bands, largely dependent on American imports, that has sown the seeds of confusion. Some of it is brash and bizarre and seems at variance with what the medium has to say. The band's ability to move widely through the various strands and styles of music gives it a diversity which sometimes tends to pull in contrary directions.

Publication of *Metamorphoses* by Edward Gregson, the first of the 'Novello Wind Band and Wind Ensemble Series', represented a bold initiative on behalf of the publishers under guidance of Timothy Reynish, the general editor. Their adventurous confidence should be rewarded by more performances as the work – scored for a minimum of thirty-six players plus basic electronics – constitutes a pertinent contribution to the repertoire. Whether more ensembles will take up the challenge *Metamorphoses* presents remains to be seen – some groups would not hesitate. Novello also undertook the publication of Holst's *Marching Song* in the composer's own scoring for small British military band.

Over the years a few internationally renowned composers have contributed to the repertoire, though the quality of some of these works is arguable. Naturally wind bands impose limitations on composers, though no more so than any other ensemble. Paradoxically, when composers elect to limit themselves to a particular medium, it appears to channel rather than restrict their creative effort. There are kitsch pieces by well-known composers just as there are imaginative, interesting works by unknowns. The medium seems to bring out either the best or worst in them. However, here we are not so much concerned with the intangibilities of taste, or even whether or not the music will ultimately withstand the test of time, but rather with an attempt to show the scope of the music for band.

Spearheading the drive for new music has been the British Youth Wind Orchestra, the National Wind Band of Scotland and latterly, the British Association for Symphonic Wind Bands and Wind Ensembles. Each of them has set national precedents in commissioning new music for the medium and has brought original material to our attention again, in some cases after a long period of time.

Most of the works commissioned by the BYWO are unpublished. Details can be obtained from either The British Music Information Centre, 10 Stratford Place, London W1, or directly from the composer. They include: *Wind Symphony* (1974) by Stephen Dodgson (Boosey & Hawkes hire library); *Concerto for Wind Orchestra* (1976) by David Morgan; *Symphony No. 8 for Wind Orchestra – The Four Elements* (op. 98, 1977) by Wilfred Josephs (Basil Ramsey); *Processiones* (1979) by Leonard Salzedo (Lopés Edition); and *Scenes from an Imaginary Ballet* (1980) by Graham Williams (Chester Music hire library). Besides these the BYWO has commissioned music for clarinet choir: *Introduction and Rondo* (1972) by Leonard Salzedo (Lopés Edition); and *Epigrams from a Garden* (1977) for contralto and clarinet choir by Stephen Dodgson (Scotus).

The NWBS, under the aegis of the Scottish Amateur Music Association, has commissioned: *Matelot – A Diversion after Grieg's Soldier's Song –* (op. 68 no. 1, 1977) by Stephen Dodgson (Scotus); *Beowulf*, by Peter Naylor; *Sinfonietta* by Arthur Oldham; *Caledonian Caprice*, by David Dorward (Scotus); *The Eagle: Tone-Poem for Wind Band after Tennyson* (1976), by Stephen Dodgson (Scotus); and *Variations and Fugue on the Wee Cooper O'Fife* by Cedric Thorpe Davie (1981).

Premièred at the second annual BASBWE Conference in 1983 were two works by British composers: *Firestar* by Philip Wilby, which is an evocation of sunrise to dawn next day and uncompromising in exploiting the gamut of modern instrumental technique; and *Gallimaufry* by Guy Woolfenden (Ariel Music). The composer's flair for wind instruments has long been recognised by theatre-goers. *Gallimaufry* sounds like a Gallic derivative and is in fact a recondite word meaning 'hotch-potch' or 'medley'. The title hardly does the work justice, for, far from being merely a farrago (a compilation of tunes strung together with all the unsubtlety of dominant sevenths), it is a fascinatingly rich tapestry of Shakespearean music. Subtly-crafted, interrelated motifs movingly unfold and culminate in a brassy expansive restatement. A pot-pourri it may be, but it is also an immediately arresting work of high order and compelling originality.

Symphony of Winds by Derek Bourgeois (R. Smith), would need a pretty advanced and dexterous youth band to do it justice. Commissioned by, and whipped up for the 1981 International Conference, it comprises three movements: *Hurricane*, with gale-force wind machine *moto perpetuo*; *Zephyr*, in which aeolian peace and harmony descend on the work; and to conclude, a bracing *March Winds*. Dazzling in technique and inventiveness, the work displays more than an occasional touch of wry humour, a quality frequently present in the composer's music.

The Duke of Cambridge Suite by Adrian Cruft (Joad), was commissioned to celebrate the 125th anniversary of the Royal Military School of Music in 1982. Called after the founder of the RMSM, the suite comprises three original movements together with two diversions, *If all the World were Paper*, and another with the curious title *Gossip Greensleeves*. The latter combines *Greensleeves* with *Good Morrow Gossip Joan*. Lest the meaning be misconstrued, the word 'gossip' formerly meant neighbour.

More and more early original music is being re-issued in addition to several newly-found works. It is here that smaller bands can come into their own. There are Concerti Grossi by Telemann written for the Court at Hamburg, eighteenth-century Viennese classical *harmoniemusik* by Haydn and Mozart, and wind ensemble music from nineteenth-century France and Germany. Xerox copies of these original editions can be obtained from WINDS (an acronym for Wind Instruments New Dawn Society), Box 513, Northridge, California 91328, USA. (Apparently much of the music listed in the WINDS catalogue is unobtainable elsewhere.) One copy of each part is supplied from which extras can be made. In addition to the above, the society has scores ranging from German baroque to nineteenth-century Austrian large band works. The society boasts several coups: an 1816 Steiner publication of Beethoven's Symphony No. 7, scored for two each of oboes, clarinets, horns and bassoons (with lots of errors!) and his *Victory Symphony* (1813) originally for large band, later rescored for orchestra to become part II of *Wellington's Victory*. The editing of these works has been carried out largely by David Whitwell, whose book, *A New History of Wind Music* (The Instrumentalist Co., 1972) has done much to steer wind band conductors back into the musical mainstream.

Recent BYWO programmes testify to its concern for music of all periods. The following are too infrequently heard in this country, but are standard repertoire in America, and are assessed at a higher worth there: Mendelssohn, Overture in C, (op. 24) written when Mendelssohn was only fifteen, for resident wind players at a Baltic Spa where he was holidaying; Berlioz, *Grande Symphonie Funèbre et Triomphale*; Grieg, *Funeral March*, originally for piano but transcribed by the composer for wind band; Respighi, *Huntingtower* – Ballad for Band, written in 1932 for the American wind band conductor Goldman;

Schoenberg, *Theme and Variations* (op. 43a), commissioned by Schirmer; and Hindemith *Symphony in B flat* (1951), written at the request of the United States Army Band.

In recent times, traditional wind band marches have been played in what has become in US universities a genre convention. To take but two examples:Fillmore's *His Honor* (*sic*), edited by Fennell (Fischer); and Sousa's *The Free Lance*, edited by Revelli (Jenson) – comprising tunes from an operetta of the same name. Neither usurps the convention though both are sensitive editions, due in no small part to the carefully-pared soloistic treatment of the voices; not fundamental changes perhaps, but certainly a refreshing shift in the wind and retaining the essence of the American march idiom. Whether or not it is wrong to pare down for the concert hall marches intended essentially for open air performances is arguable, but for sheer clarity of performance alone a well-edited score which reduces the doubling and lays bare the original part writing cannot be denied.

Percy Grainger's substantial contribution to the repertoire shows something of his attraction for the medium. He once said, 'I have ceased to be a guesser and amateur as regards wind instruments.' His *Children's March, Over the Hills and Far Away*, was written whilst he was serving as a bandsman in the US Army, but his classic, *A Lincolnshire Posy* (a setting of six folk songs collected by the composer), is especially revealing. Interleaving the digital recording by the Cleveland Symphonic Winds conducted by Frederick Fennell, with original phonograph recordings made by the folk singers in Lincolnshire from whom Grainger gathered his material during the first decade of the century, makes interesting study. Placed side by side in this way the comparison is particularly germane, revealing Grainger not only as probably the most original orchestrator of the medium (a view widely held in any case) but also showing him to have a complete rapport with the spirit of the original. The arrangements and rhapsodic treatments transcend every nuance of the words, from melancholic inflexion to alcoholic elation.

Generally, English folk music is well represented in the repertoire. Best-known are the two military band suites in E flat and F by Holst, written in 1909 and 1911 respectively, and the *English Folk Song Suite* by Vaughan Williams, scored at the request of Col. Somerville for Kneller Hall in the 1920s, though the songs themselves were collected earlier. Played rather less often are *Toccata Marziale* by Vaughan Williams, Holst's *Hammersmith* and *Old Wine in New Bottles*, a set of four folk songs arranged by Gordon Jacob who, incidentally, transcribed the Vaughan Williams' *Folk-Song Suite* for orchestra. Recently re-issued are the *Three Dale Dances* by Wood arranged by Maas

(Molenaar), though some will tend to spurn them because of their brass band associations. The longevity of folk-song arrangements is understandable; more difficult to comprehend is that they seem to have import for audiences almost everywhere.

That hardy perennial of the repertoire, Holst's *First Suite in E flat*, could never become a tired old piece, though it may sometimes be played in a tired old way. We who interpret, have to learn to shape the space within Holst's framework. In accordance with his direction in the original score, the suite should be 'played right through without a break'. The autograph full score can be found in the British Library Department of Manuscripts (Additional MS 47824), though it goes without saying that for performance of the original scoring, permission of the copyright holders must be obtained.

The same composer's deft brushstrokes and range of tonal palette are apparent within the seemingly transparent but really iridescent orchestral texture of *Hammersmith*, at once hauntingly familiar and evocative. Music intended for professionals – the BBC Military Band – it has to be played with the requisite professional ease. At a recent performance of *Hammersmith*, another English composer, Joseph Horovitz, remarked 'Now that's what I call a really modern piece of music.' Indeed, many would accord with such a viewpoint. *Hammersmith* was, and is today, regarded as totally original music in tune with the mood of the time. We in Britain ought to appreciate our unique position in having a work to play of this order. Whilst the contribution English composers have made to wind band repertoire may hardly be considered substantial quantitatively, the quality of such works as the Holst *Suites*, or *Hammersmith*; Vaughan Williams' *Folk Song Suite* or *Toccata Marziale*; and *An Original Suite* by Gordon Jacob, would seem irrefutable. At the time Gordon Jacob wrote his *Original Suite* (1923), so little music was being written for military band that the chosen title was a way of distinguishing that it was an original work, not an arrangement, and that the tunes though 'folkish' were the composer's own.

Building a library of music is expensive, particularly as much of the music is dependent on the American publishing houses. It is vital, therefore, that the music pays its way. Several local education authorities have tackled this problem by organising a central wind band music library. As an extension of this, schools have submitted lists of their own libraries to a central point, and a complete graded catalogue is then circularised within that authority. This seems an admirable scheme provided that strict copyright procedure is followed. At one time there was a specialist wind music hire library in Britain but, alas, it no longer exists. The Americans have a contemporary music library, comprising scores and parts originally written for school performing groups. Copies of these may be borrowed in Britain for a loan period of up to two months and in some cases, recorded performances are available. The catalogue lists the suggested level of performance from college and advanced high school to junior high and elementary, as well as grading within these broad bands.

Finally, further repertoire suggestions can be found in *Band Music Guide* (Instrumentalist Co., Illinois); *Composer*, magazine of the British Music Information Centre; *More Ideas for Wind Orchestra* by Geoffrey Emerson (Emerson Edition); *The Trumpeter* (NSBA) and the *Journal of the British Association of Symphonic Wind Bands and Wind Emsembles*.

Part IV BRASS BAND

11 An introduction

To many people brass band instruments and their nomenclature are perplexing in the extreme. Mention has already been made of some of the instruments: the cornet, conically-bored, capable of being played with greater deftness and more rounded in tone than the strident, cylindrically-bored trumpet of the orchestra; the baritone, slighter and lighter-toned than the euphonium with which it shares the same pitch; and the E flat tenor horn – really an alto saxhorn – gossamer-like, with more transparency than its orchestral counterpart but lacking the French horn's vast compass.

The piccolo of the brass band is the soprano cornet in E flat. Played well, it has a wispy, flute-like quality, in contrast to the more rounded B flat cornets. The flugel horn – ostensibly a valved bugle – has a larger, more conical bore than that of the cornet and in consequence is mellower in tone. Although of the same pitch as the cornet, it is, as its name suggests, essentially a horn with a forward-facing bell. But it is with the tubas, or basses as they are known in brass band parlance, that much confusion arises. Briefly, there are two types of basses: the smaller E flat and the larger B flat variety. Mostly they play in octaves, in unison, and occasionally in fifths. The full complement can be seen below. The usual doublings are shown in parentheses.

Brass band instrumentation: full complement
soprano cornet in E flat
solo cornets in B flat   (from three to five players)
ripieno cornet in B flat
second cornets in B flat   (two players)
third cornets in B flat   (two players)

flugel horn in B flat
solo (tenor) horn in E flat
first (tenor) horn in E flat
second (tenor) horn in E flat

first baritone in B flat
second baritone in B flat

first trombone in B flat
second trombone in B flat
bass trombone in C

euphoniums in B flat	(two players)
basses in E flat	(two players)
basses in B flat	(two players)
percussion	(two players)

The term 'repiano' is a mis-spelt derivative of 'ripieno' and should be properly called that, though only one publisher continues to do so. Distorted though the term may be, the part fulfils a useful purpose within the scoring scheme. Placed between the solo and second cornet registers, it can fill out the three-part chordal structure, or, when not treated soloistically as an independent voice, can be used, especially in *divisi* passages, simply to strengthen the existing lines.

The 'solo' horn, a term which distinguishes the player as a soloist, is fitly named. Like the term 'ripieno', it owes much to seventeenth- and eighteenth-century concerti grossi in which a single, principal part would be referred to as 'solo' rather than 'concertante' (a group of soloists). Why the other two horn parts should be known as 'first' and 'second' and not as 'second' and 'third', respectively, is a curious datum the reason for which is lost in the origins of the brass band. Other than for pacifying consequential rank-and-file players, there seems little logic in the practice. Incidentally, in Salvation Army scores the cornet parts, divided into three distinct lines, are labelled in the same way.

Not only is the brass band more homogeneous than the wind band, but its size and instrumentation are more stable. But the very uniformity of the brass band and its apparent resistance to extending the range of its tonal palette, may in time cause it to be viewed as an anachronism. Until recently its stylistic practices and tone were incompatible with orchestral brass playing. Even casual listeners were conscious of the differences: they were often more conscious of differences than of resemblances. Nowadays, however, due in no small part to the influence of orchestral trumpeters coaching bands, the overall sound of the brass band has been brought closer to the timbre of the orchestral brass, so much so that with some transcriptions it is hard to differentiate between the two. Although generally the accent may still be that of the brass band, there are now signs of orchestral overlay.

Discussion over the possibility of French horns replacing the E flat tenor horns, and the use of the trumpet, the E flat or piccolo B flat, in place of the soprano cornet, could be taken as signalling a fundamental change of attitude, if such discussion had not taken place before; Russell and Elliot were making much the same point in the thirties. Nevertheless, there have been some attempts at widening the instrumentation, most notably by the London Collegiate Brass which has inaugurated the new tone. Its use of French horns, challenging convention and effectively 'orchestralising' the ensemble, has met with cries of adulteration from dyed-in-the-wools unreceptive to new ideas and determined to preserve the traditional line-up. Changing attitudes are not dominant notes of the movement. But what are the positive aspects of having a standardised, homogeneous instrumentation, apart from authenticity for authenticity's sake? Basically they would seem to be three-fold.

In the first place, the instruments are so closely related that transfer from one instrument to another is relatively straightforward. A player, perhaps experiencing embouchure difficulties on the cornet, may change quickly to the tenor horn without having to read a different clef or learn a new set of finger patterns.

In the second place, composers, arrangers and publishers know precisely the make-up of the band, the parts that are likely to be doubled, and in the case of educationally-based bands, approximately the degree of surmountable difficulty between the various component parts. In the brass band there is not only a natural progression of skills whereby players can move up or down the band according to their standard, but also clearly defined divisions of those skills, so the problem of different standards within a band can be overcome, to some extent, by a natural division of labour. Published school band music seldom makes the same technical demands of second and third cornet players as of solo cornet players; there is a series of graduated steps.

Finally, the sheer homogeneity of the brass band, coupled with similarity of technique, identical fingering patterns, and – excepting bass trombone – the use of treble clef across the entire range of instruments, lends itself readily to group tuition. Moreover, for group lessons the band can be divided into two or three viable sub-groups, B flat, E flat and trombones – treble clef trombonists are frequently incorporated within the B flat group. Indeed, although the practice is less common in schools today, some years ago it was not unusual for one person to teach every member of the band. Private or individual lessons were almost unheard of. Most players were taught the basics in small groups, and then placed next to someone more experienced in the band. Learning from others, a practice which formerly was used extensively in industry, and known colloquially as 'sitting next to Nelly', was a key process factor.

In the case of the brass band, parallels with industry are especially pertinent. Some might say that professional orchestral players from this kind of background are remarkable not because of early group playing but in spite of it. Anyone who has undergone this kind of learning will know that it is casual, opportunistic; learning advances tend to come irregularly – but then they do in any case. It can also be an expedient, enjoyable mode of learning. What is experienced can often be retained in a way that solitary learning cannot, undoubtedly because of the social context in which it takes place, and because the experiences are share-able. It is as if such shared experiences stimulate the mind in a way that is different from individual learning. It turns you out of yourself.

12 The embryonic brass band

Whilst opinions vary as to the most useful instrumentation with which to start a school brass band, it is wise to cover the four basic parts – soprano, alto, tenor and bass. Cornets take the soprano line; lower cornets and horns the alto; horns, baritones or trombones supply the tenor voices; whilst the bass line may be played by euphoniums, trombones, or basses proper. A quartet comprising: two cornets, horn and euphonium, or alternatively, any combination of instruments drawn from the band within the same four basic registers can form the nucleus of a brass band, though it should be said that published arrangements and compositions are restricted, and tend to be more readily available for the standard quartet.

	Division of parts
Soprano	cornets
Alto	cornets, flugel horn, tenor horns
Tenor	tenor horns, baritones, trombones
Bass	euphoniums, E flat and B flat basses, bass trombone

Additional instruments may make feasible a quintet: two cornets, tenor horn, trombone and E flat bass; a septet: two cornets, tenor horn, baritone, trombone, euphonium and E flat bass; or a decet: four cornets, tenor horn, trombone, bass trombone, euphonium, E flat bass and percussion. A number of publishers issue scores and parts for these ensembles but, in beginner and elementary stages of the ensemble, it is likely that the teacher would need to supplement the available repertoire with his or her own arrangements. Balanced ratios of instruments to ensembles can be seen more clearly in the table on page 102.
Note that, except in the full complement, the soprano cornet has been omitted. It is unlikely that there will be a need for such a player until the final stages – in any case anyone other than the most discreet, sensitive player can mar an otherwise reasonable band. If the instrument is conspicuous by its absence, it would be more so by its presence in the hands of an indifferent player.

Balanced ratios of instruments to ensembles

	quartet	quintet	septet	decet	full band
soprano cornet					1
cornets	2	2	2	4	8–10
flugel horn					1
tenor horns	1	1	1	1	3
baritones				1	2
tenor trombones		1	1	1	2
bass trombone				1	1
euphoniums	1		1	1	2
E flat basses		1	1	1	2
B flat basses					2
percussion				1	2

Some teachers prefer to delay the addition of trombones until the band is beyond the embryonic stage. The writer's personal preference is to involve trombonists in the ensemble from the outset, because then they are less likely to lag behind the other, valve-instrument players. Moreover, they gain valuable ensemble experience which in turn helps their intonation.

Mouthpieces, instruments and embouchure

The need for compatible mouthpieces and instruments cannot be over-stressed. Too often instruments of reasonable quality are played with inferior or incompatible, ill-fitting mouthpieces. Generally speaking, European instruments should be played with matching European mouthpieces; American mouthpieces with the American-made instruments for which they are intended. Although European and American mouthpieces and instruments might appear interchangeable, in practice it is unwise to mix the two as doing so usually adversely affects the player's intonation. Whilst it may not be possible to see at a glance a mouthpiece unsuitable for the instrument with which it is being used, it is possible to hear one. In the same way, it may not be possible to see a poor embouchure, especially with players of larger instruments, but it is possible to hear the product of one.

As one player's embouchure is so radically different from that of another's, it would be as unwise to give advice on the 'correct' placement of the mouthpiece, as it would be to generalise on its size or on the type of instrument suitable for this or that person. Contradictions are legion; sound and comfort are the only meaningful criteria.

Seating

Well-placed, favourably situated players contribute to sensitive, musical performances. Three types of seating formation predominate today: traditional seating, known as concert formation (fig. 1); broadcasting formation, arrived at by the BBC in the late thirties (fig. 2); and a third, more recent arrangement whereby the former and latter are fused together (fig. 3). These are not immutable; bands do, of course, re-arrange slightly depending on personal preferences and the overall balance of the sections concerned, but generally, seating is not far removed from one of the three types illustrated.

Figure 1

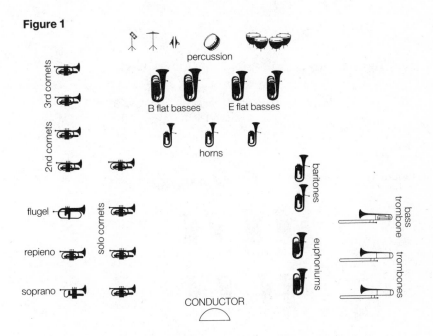

Figure 2

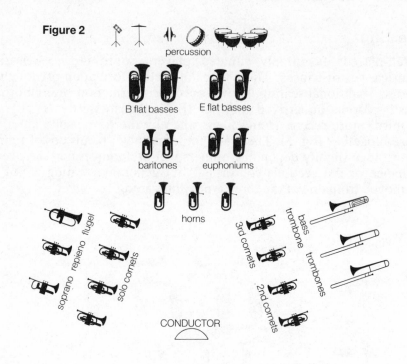

percussion

B flat basses   E flat basses

baritones   euphoniums

horns

soprano   repiano   flugel   solo cornets   3rd cornets   2nd cornets   trombones   bass trombone

CONDUCTOR

Figure 3

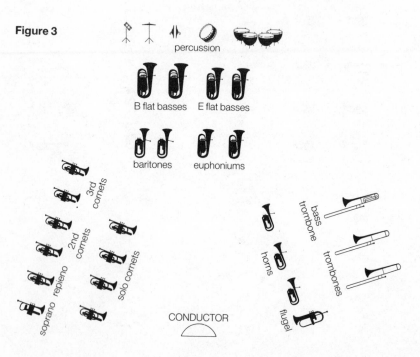

percussion

B flat basses   E flat basses

baritones   euphoniums

soprano   repiano   3rd cornets   2nd cornets   solo cornets   horns   flugel   trombones   bass trombone

CONDUCTOR

Pros and cons, largely to do with the position of the euphonium, are apparent in each. The euphonium is an anchor. More than any other instrument it gives the brass band its characteristic quality of sound. In concert formation, it is in the foreground to project important melodic lines, but because it is essentially a bass, it is too far placed from the other basses to blend. Positioned directly forward of the E flat basses so that all the bells point in one direction, it mixes well, but given a tenor countermelody (as the euphonium so often is) some of the clarity of musical line which is discernible when the instrument is facing the cornets is impaired. Moreover, placing the cornets and trombones together, or merely positioning the trombones on the conductor's right, a penchant some bands have developed of late, can make for too harsh a timbre without the euphonium or horns brought forward to add mellowness and absorb some of the stridency.

Rather than adopting a lay-out once and for all, the band should regularly take time to experiment and assess others. Much will depend on the timbre for which the members are aiming, and the kind of programme being rehearsed. Whatever seating plan is being used, there is much to be said for diagonally angling the positions of the players seated to the conductor's left and right, thus narrowing the band at the top to form an inverted funnel shape with the percussion at the vertex.

13   Rehearsals

It is essential that the players warm their instruments prior to rehearsal, irrespective of whether the conductor chooses to start with a communal warm-up or not. Once 'played in' the instruments should be kept warm to ensure that the tuning remains stable and the attack secure. Too often players enter flat after only a few bars rest. A cold instrument will tend to play flat becoming progressively sharper as it warms: an overheated atmosphere will make the instruments excessively sharp.

Even the most expensive instruments are seldom absolutely in tune throughout the entire register. Certain acknowledged suspect notes, inherent in all brass instruments, have been touched upon earlier. Each player should come to know which notes on his or her own instrument require coaxing; either bringing up or levelling down to correct pitch.

Intonation and tone quality go hand in hand. Bright, sharp-toned players can be mellowed by changing to mouthpieces with deeper cups. Conversely, dull, flat-toned players can be brightened by using mouthpieces with shallower cups. Some difficulties in tone production, however, though far from insuperable, are less easily disposed of.

A 'steamy', breathy sound is usually caused by air escaping from the corners of the player's lips rather than, as might be supposed, from leaks in the instrument. Consequently, cornet players, because of their small, comparatively shallow mouthpieces, are more prone to producing breathy sounds than most, especially in the upper register. The players concerned should learn to seal the parts of their lips either side of the mouthpiece firmly. Sometimes a mouthpiece with a slightly deeper cup, which allows the column of air to be channelled more easily into the instrument, can help.

A 'thin' tone is a sure sign of insufficient breath support, often combined with the player applying excessive mouthpiece pressure. Because the player fails to fill the instrument, the resultant sound is less rich in overtones than it should be. Underplaying is harder to correct than overblowing, which can be remedied in a relatively simple manner by using greater restraint, by changing to a deeper, less resistant mouthpiece, or by playing on an instrument which speaks easily and is more

106

responsive. Thin-toned players have really to return to first principles. They should learn to apply less pressure on the lips (almost without exception the top lip) and to breathe more deeply from the diaphragm. Sometimes, changing to a smaller instrument may help, but given breathing exercises regularly, there is little reason why a full-bodied sound cannot be achieved within the space of a few weeks.

Incorrect, shallow breathing, as distinct from using the diaphragm, can give rise, also, to an uncontrolled, quivering sound and may prevent the player from ending phrases artistically. Again, breathing exercises – preferably with the player seated, keeping the body straight, inhaling deeply and slowly – together with long note practice, should help.

Endurance

The tendency in most rehearsals is to play too much and listen too little, but in rehearsing an all-brass combination, allowing sufficient non-playing time is a necessity. Young or inexperienced brass players tend to fatigue quickly. A break in playing – perhaps deploying another section of the band yet keeping the rest aurally aware and alert by giving them something specific to listen for – can act as a welcome rejuvenator.

Endurance is, of course, related to musculature, the amount of practice the player has had prior to rehearsal, diaphragm support, atmospheric temperature and humidity, and the intensity and volume of playing. Poor intonation involving an individual, or the players around him, constantly having to lip the notes into pitch, or perhaps using more tension in the lip muscles than is necessary, resulting in a sharp high register, will also reduce stamina. Unstrained players should remain in pitch through to the end of a long rehearsal; flagging players will become flat, so the conductor's ear should tell him or her when to change tack.

Tuning

Again, the main tuning should take place not at the commencement of a rehearsal, but when the instruments are warm and the players 'lipped in' – that is they have had the opportunity of playing themselves in. To this end, it is common practice to start with a hymn or a march. What-ever is chosen, it ought not to exert the players; they should reserve their stamina for the main body of the rehearsal. This first piece then, may serve as a communal warm-up, but a musical one nonetheless, with as much attention given to details of expression and phrasing as the ensuing pieces. Proficient, sensitive musicians will be able to detect minor faults in intonation, make the necessary slight adjustments, and carry out much of the preliminary tuning during this first piece. Inexperienced players will need more time and patience. The conductor may have to assist them in deciding whether or not their sounds need to be flattened or sharpened, particularly where the difference in pitch is fractional. Although ultimately the conductor will assume responsibility for the overall intonation of the band, each player must accept responsibility for the tuning of his or her own instrument. Each must learn to tune efficiently, learn when and how to adjust the tuning slides, know accurately the degree to which they need to be pushed in for the sounds to become sharper and pulled out to become flatter. Every player should learn how to tune as soon as possible, as a violinist or guitarist would. As the pitch of brass instruments fluctuates less widely than that of strings, the process of learning to tune them is, in many instances, habitually postponed.

In orchestras and in chamber music ensembles, tuning is a prerequisite for rehearsal. Throughout an orchestral rehearsal, or public performance, there are frequent interim checks. Indeed, the idea of playing without first the entire orchestra or ensemble tuning is inconceivable. In bands, collective tuning often takes place only when the conductor insists upon it. Careful tuning should be a matter of course. Every member must go through the process of tuning in relation to the rest of the players each time that the band convenes. It is the only solution to the problem of poor intonation in our bands; the only way to cultivate in band members instinctive, critical listening to their own and to their colleagues' playing.

But from whom should we take our pitch? As a general rule, the smaller the instrument the greater the inherent tuning problems, and the less likely it is to intone the correct pitch; this is one reason why many American wind ensembles tune to the tuba – a practice which has much to commend it. Another opinion holds that we should identify the person in the band who plays flattest – when all the tuning slides are pushed home – and for him, or her, to set the pitch. The explanation for this approach is clear: namely, that by sufficiently extending their tuning slides the rest of the members of the band can tune down to this player. Again, a commendable approach. But there are, it should be remembered, degrees of flatness, and in school bands comprising young, inexperienced players, the gradations are steeper than most. We should be reluctant to tune the band to anything less than concert pitch. Apart from the effect it might have on the others, it is unlikely that a player who unconsciously plays so very flat could be relied upon to produce a stable, steady pitch time and time again whilst every member of the band tunes. Better, surely, to attempt to bring such a player more in tune with the sounds of the rest of the band by a change of mouthpiece or instrument.

Whether we choose to start the tuning from the person who plays the flattest, from the basses, from the cornets (a time-honoured way), or the trombones (generally considered the most reliable of all the pitch makers), the only hard and fast rule is that each player should sound an open note. For clarity, let us suppose we commence with the cornets and work down through the various sections to the basses (but reversing the order would be an equally valid approach; perhaps more valid).

Sounding unison B flat is a simple way of brass band tuning: firstly, each player plays in turn, followed by the separate sections, concluding with the full band. Written, middle register C and G (sounding B flat) are played by B flat and E flat instruments respectively. Alternatively, or as a secondary measure, still using open notes, the band can tune in fourths and fifths sounding by turn B flat and F (E flat instruments playing G, B flat instruments C and G). Should it be felt necessary to complete the chord by adding a major third, it is unwise to give it to the B flat instruments because written low E (first line of the stave) is slightly sharp, the upper (fourth space) slightly flat. It is more tuneful to allocate the third to the horns; they read B and sound D.

Provided that each instrument is in tune with itself – excepting those notes inherently sharp or flat which have to be humoured – the general level of intonation should be respectable. In practice, however, it is likely that some will be out of tune with themselves and the players must set about tuning the valve slides, a task which is not as formidable as it may at first seem. Each player must go through alternative fingerings, paying particular attention to the third valve which needs to be in tune with the notes produced more usually by depressing first and second valves. The combinations: first and second; first and third; first, second and third; tend towards sharpness. Although the amount by which the valve slides are lengthened will be proportionate to how far the main tuning slide is extended, it is unlikely that the small second valve slide will need adjustment. The slide is so very short that it makes the effect of adjustment if not infinitesimal then, with a sensitive ear and flexible embouchure, of little practical consequence. With the first and third valve slides, however, the difference in pitch when either is extended is marked.

The point – you will notice – to which we keep returning is that valved brass instruments, refined as they are, cannot be made to sound every note in their range absolutely in tune simply by depressing the valves and playing regardlessly. And whilst most of the finer tuning has to be consciously carried out by the player, some of it will be effected subconsciously. Even to equal-tempered ears the same note in one key will sound flatter or sharper when played in another. Take for example B played in the sequences G A B and A B C sharp. Subconsciously, the players will correctly sharpen the second B more than the first. Similarly, if intoned as a dominant seventh and then as a leading note.

Some less conscious influences are detrimental to good tuning and ought to be mentioned. In the first place, no player can possibly be accurately tuned to another if, when he tunes, he applies anything more than natural vibrato. At best he can only approximate his intonation, as in effect his pitch will constantly oscillate between flatness and sharpness. In the second place, the players should not assume that an instrument formerly in tune will remain so when muted. Mutes tend to sharpen the pitch in addition to sharpening the tone. In the third place, players overblowing – possibly most common along the front row – will appear to be tuned rather sharply; those underplaying, the reverse.

Although some notes can be adjusted only by the embouchure, others such as low C sharp, D, F sharp and G may be corrected on some instruments by an adjustable ring, saddle or trigger, which enables the player to extend the third and, increasingly today, the first valve slides; or by a system of extra tubing known as compensating valves. But whether compensating by embouchure or with the aid of mechanical devices, the player's ear has to be sufficiently developed to tell him or her when, and how much, adjustment is necessary. And that, a matter of aural awareness, is the essence of tuning and intonation.

Balance

One fourteenth-century visitor to Britain remarked, on returning to his place of origin, that the Britons are 'vastly fond of great noises'. Does the maxim still hold true today? If it does it is a question not of volume but of balance. In any ensemble the overall unity of volume is a matter for every single player. A well-balanced brass band is imposing in its volume but balance is dependent on unity.

In the cornet section the more technically demanding passages are usually assigned to the most dexterous players: the solo cornets. These front row, tutti cornet players (colloquially known as the 'bumpers-up', the term is not inappropriate) play the heavy, taxing passages leaving the principal cornettist fresh for the soloistic sections. Co-operating as a team by turn-taking works well, but when there are many players – and there may be up to five – doubling the solo cornet line, the band can easily become unbalanced. Here again, there should be a division of labour. Playing as a group, the solo cornet players can sound as one: playing as individuals with distinctive sounds or styles, they vie with one another to be heard above the rest. As with the rest of the band, they should develop a concept of ensemble playing with regard to balance, blend, intonation and tone quality, not a windmilling disregard for everyone else. Playing in a band involves a group effort; save for solo passages, it should be difficult to hear a particular individual.

Whereas in the wind band, restraint in heavily scored passages may well be more the concern of the brass than of the woodwind, in the brass band because the instruments are fairly matched dynamically, each player must attend meticulously to tonal balance and to the fine and not so fine points of proportion. Though the brass band is a harmonious and essentially monochrome ensemble, there are some unequal tones. The heraldic colour of the cornets and trombones, for instance, will need to be held in check, as will the sonorous, sombre-toned euphoniums and basses, against the soft-hued horns and baritones. Whilst the wind band is inordinately well-supplied with flutes, clarinets and trumpets which make it top heavy, the brass band, with its preponderance of tenor voices, trombones, baritones and euphoniums, is almost the reverse. Neither has the tonal, intrinsic equilibrium of the orchestra or is so ideally attuned to accompanying itself. Admittedly, disparity between the various sections can be redressed by marshalling our forces and levelling up or down accordingly (such points can be worked out in rehearsal) but, in terms of instrumentation, brass bands and wind bands lack internal balance of proportion. We should rethink our assumptions and view the ensembles not as balanced, but tend to the contrary belief that balance has to be externally imposed.

Articulation

Articulation has already been discussed briefly with regard to wind band rehearsal points, but how does it differ, if at all, within the brass band setting? In the brass band the hard, strongly accented attack, so characteristic of the orchestral brass, is less effective than in the orchestra, or in the wind band where such parts would be better assigned to trumpets and trombones than cornets. As a consequence of the instruments having deeper, funnel-shaped mouthpieces, overall the brass band has less bite, yet the instruments can enter with more subtlety and are capable of producing a soft, liquid sound. But while conscious that the sounds produced are different, we may be more conscious of the resemblances in the production of the sounds. In producing the notes the tongue should not strike but withdraw. For players to grasp this idea more firmly – for many the placement and action of the tongue has an air of abstraction – it is worth translating it into more concrete or familiar terms.

A favourite analogy among brass teachers for the action of the tongue, is that of a tap controlling water flow. Just as a tap releases the flow of water, so the tongue releases a flow of air. However, to extend the analogy, unfortunately some players use the tongue not so much as a tap to turn off the supply of air, stopping it smoothly, quickly and silently, but as a plug by placing it between the lips – a habit which dies hard. Once the source of the problem has been identified, the players should practise stopping the sound by placing the tongue behind the top teeth.

Quality of articulation, both of attack and release, is as fundamental to brass playing as clear enunciation is to speech. In speech, we learn to enunciate by listening to others talk: in music, we learn to articulate by listening to others play. Modelling in the brass band is rife; the technique of tone production on the instruments is, after all, the same. Of course, a player must listen to good tone production in order to know what is expected, but he or she may learn also by hearing faults in some-one else's playing. When we listen to a successful speech we may be too carried away by the content or by the sheer fluency of the speaker to analyse it properly. Similarly, when we listen to a stunning perform-ance, the musicianship and the virtuosity of the performer make it difficult to stand back and dispassionately appraise it. We can learn much from listening critically when a speaker, or the performer, in this case, is disappointing. What advice could we give him? What is wrong with the way he produces the sounds? By posing such questions it is likely that the players themselves will already have gone part of the way to improving their own tone production, because the first step to finding fault in their own playing is to find fault in other people's. Laying bare their own efforts is to take the second step.

14 Writing for brass band

The present chapter does not attempt to thumb-nail brass band scoring but is concerned, unashamedly, with a few of the problems among many that are encountered when writing (either composing or arranging) for brass and more particularly, with the practical points to be borne in mind when writing for young, or inexperienced brass players. And if it fans the desire to commit something to paper, or merely to delve deeper into the subject, it is all to the good. Writing for brass band not only means knowing the conventions, but also knowing when to take liberties. As before, the text is interlarded with musical quotations to illuminate the various points.

Much of the material quoted is perennial, drawing on indigenous folk song, though the examples are not restricted exclusively to pieces in a folkloristic idiom. The examples are not held up as models of scoring – merely as options. Being relatively simple to handle, folk songs make a fitting starting point, and have the additional advantage of being both readily and freely available for transcription. Besides, as regards scoring folk song material, the brass band has yet to find its Lincolnshire Posy.

Composers and arrangers writing for band have drawn and will continue to draw, on folk songs as is inevitable with such familiar material; each finding different ways of setting them. The options are almost inexhaustible. The biggest temptation at a more advanced level is to set them with a sophistication wholly incommensurate with the simplicity of the songs themselves. What was envisaged as a simple, sparse accompaniment can fructify like ivy on a cottage wall, until it threatens to overwhelm the structure to which it is appended.

Today, whilst there is a wealth of pieces cleverly arranged for brass bands of advanced standard, there would seem to be considerably less material suitable for those of an intermediate grade – the more capable school and music centre bands. Many of the compositionally adventurous pieces tend also to be difficult technically, though there are notable exceptions. 'Bespoke' arrangements can fill a useful rôle both in bridging the gap between advanced and elementary music, and in pitching the level of the parts to suit the intended players. With a music centre

113

band that is larger than usual, music can be written or arranged to exploit its size, perhaps breaking down the full band into separate instrumental choirs. Such arrangements can also include parts that are not normally included in the standard set such as parts for French horns, bass clef trombones, baritones, euphoniums and basses. Lower brass players in orchestras and wind bands, when turning to brass band, have to learn to read treble clef. Whilst that may be a valuable exercise in itself, should we not offer such players a choice of clefs as some publishers do? If only more published scores aimed at school and music centre bands included alternative parts it would save much of the time teachers presently spend in re-writing. In educationally-based bands, where the emphasis should be on involving as many students as possible, the complete instrumentation with extra parts may be as follows:

soprano   (could be played by E flat trumpet)
solo cornets
ripieno
second cornets
third cornets
flugel horn
solo horn   ⎫
first horn   ⎬   or French horns
second horn   ⎭
first baritone   ⎫
second baritone   ⎪
first trombone   ⎪
second trombone   ⎬   with alternative bass clef parts
bass trombone   ⎪
euphoniums   ⎪
E flat basses   ⎪
B flat basses   ⎭
percussion

The score would show only the traditional instrumentation as the extra parts need not be independent; merely transpositions of existing ones. In the published edition of *Praeludium* by Philip Lane (1982), alternative parts are provided within the standard set.

Whilst on the subject of scores, it should be mentioned that there is little point in making a piano reduction. Since a full score is necessary to rehearse the piece properly, it might as well be made in the throes of composition, or at the time of conceiving the arrangement, than be copied out afterwards from separate parts. Moreover, a piece by a relatively inexperienced composer or arranger is often more professionally wrought from a full score. It may take more time to prepare but the result is usually worth the extra effort. In the long run the piece will be easier to rehearse and, in consequence, ought to be better performed.

As all the instruments are pitched naturally in either B flat or E flat, the brass band is given to flat rather than sharp keys: written C, F, B flat and G (sounding a tone lower) being the most tuneful.

In comparison with the kaleidoscopic tone quality of the wind band, the brass band is decidedly monochrome. To make a simile with the imitative arts, the brass band can be likened to a charcoal drawing. But just as we might elect to use only primary colours within the tonal spectrum when scoring for wind band, we may choose to separate the tonal shades within the range of an all-brass combination. Since the brass band is a homogeneous ensemble, it is as well, in first setting out to score for brass band, to opt for well-contrasted tonal groups: perhaps the brightly-toned cornets and trombones against the mellow saxhorns. Separating such sharply-defined sonorities gives clarity to the collective timbre and prevents it merging into sombre-toned opaqueness. Thus tonal separation, isolating contrasting groups, is an effective way of bringing light and shade into a brass band score and avoids a mishmash of texture. So the first dictum about brass band scoring is: know the tonal groups.

As a springboard to other scoring techniques, let us examine tonal separation in greater detail looking at a number of contrasting groups within the complete brass band. It is a sort of Russian doll approach: inside each one there is another. The list of examples is far from exhaustive. Those that follow are merely some of the possible combinations and permutations. First, groups of like instruments which may be scored independently.

Scoring cornets as a separate tonal entity is an effective ploy though isolating any group more than occasionally will sound piecemeal and inexpert. In the simple setting shown in example 1 on page 117, alternate answering phrases are passed from plaintive saxhorns to the more sanguine cornets. Lower saxhorns, comprising euphoniums and baritones, are well-grouped provided that the lower parts are not too closely spaced. Here, their elegiac quality is quite in character with the sentiment of the folk song.

With the same proviso about spacing, the basses may be given up to four separate parts. In the following example, based on 'What Shall we do with the Drunken Sailor', the melody is played by muted soprano cornet underpinned by a three-part bass accompaniment: euphonium, E flat and B flat bass. Baritones sustain and bind the texture:

Close harmony suitably placed for horn quartet with the flugel taking the melody line can sound especially sensuous. In practical terms, however, the horn range is somewhat restricting so voicings will need to be carefully moulded. Example 2 on pages 118–19 shows how this can work.

Sometimes the harmony will need to be more widely spaced, especially where the horns are assigned to a supportive role. As a general rule, however, it is unwise to write below middle C for horns, their intonation in this part of the register being notoriously unreliable.

For purity of cylindrical tones, the trombone trio may be scored independently, as in the following example based on 'I'se the B'y that Builds the Boat':

Example 1:

Leave Her, Johnny, Leave Her

arr. K. Thompson

Example 2:
Shenandoah

arr. K. Thompson

Alternatively, it may be subtly fused with baritone to make up a four-some. In the adagio of example 2 the basses move at each phrase end giving rhythmic impetus whilst trombones and baritone sustain close harmonies; the latter supplies the sevenths.

Even if the range of tonal contrast is greater than it might first appear, the essence of a composition or transcription should not be wholly colouristic. It is hard, for example, to conceive of *La Mer* for brass band. Of course, the symbolism of colour – apparent in Gilbert Vinter's *Spectrum*, for instance – rather than the suggestion of colour itself is quite a different matter.

Many arrangers scoring for band seem reluctant to write rests with the result that everyone is playing all the time. Except in passages where the arranger wants specifically the full band to come together, say, to increase the intensity of the piece at a certain point, it is better to err on the side of economy, using four and five voices at a time, than bring the others, bleating melodiously, into the same fold. Apart from the absurdity of writing subsidiary parts just to keep the others playing, bear in mind that young, inexperienced brass players tire easily, so in a piece of any length rests ought not to be too infrequent. For similar reasons, instead of several players doubling the same lines, occasionally the direction 'one player per part' can give the ensemble playing a delicacy akin to chamber music, and the others respite during which time they can direct their attention to listening. Since a full complement is common, there is less need to cue extensively than when scoring for wind band.

All the parts should be placed within the comfortable compass of the instruments, either by avoiding extremities completely, or including alternative middle-range cues. Even if the uppermost notes of the register (top A, B and C) are avoided, if the overall lie of the parts remains high, players will find them surprisingly tiring. Care then should be taken to vary the register as often as is feasible. If scoring for a band without a soprano player, essential parts may be cued in the solo cornet copy, marking them 'one only'. Writing for a young or inexperienced soprano cornet player demands considerable thought and attention. It is unwise to use the player merely to support the front row cornets in their high register or to have the soprano soaring head and shoulders above the rest, unless the player happens to have excessive sang-froid coupled with consistent coruscating form. A high soprano may claim attention and be exhilirating to hear, but it is wiser and safer to regard the instrument as having a similar quality of expression to that of the flute rather than that of the piccolo when writing for school and music centre. The instrument is light as opposed to shrill, and may therefore be used in transparently-scored passages, perhaps where the full-bodied, rounded tone of the B flat cornet would be out of character.

Apart from optional (ossia) high and low notes, scores wrought by the teacher can include more *divisi* parts than is usually the case in published editions. As was suggested when discussing writing for oboes and alto saxophones in the wind band, when writing in the high register for brass band solo cornets, it is preferable for reasons of intonation to divide the single line part.

Again intricate passages are made easier when divided and 'dovetailed'. Although the practice is commonplace between the solo cornets, their part may also be divided with the soprano as in the following example based on 'A-Roving'. A phrase conceived:

can be written in a slightly modified form:

Demanding passages are usually assigned to the four 'corner' players, namely: solo cornet, horn, euphonium and first trombone. But even if the other parts are made less difficult, it is better to keep them interesting so that the rest of the players may also improve at a steady pace. The emphasis here is on couching the parts less awkwardly as distinct from making them unchallengingly simple. On occasion, that may be a fine distinction to draw, for any but accomplished composers and arrangers. Given that the inside parts are more restricted in range, they can still be stimulating to play provided that the arranger makes them so. The players should be challenged, not coddled; that could only ever be counterproductive. Moreover, if we are to depart at all from the type of scoring whereby most of the players play most of the time, as is the brass band's wont, then the 'rank and file' ought not to be made to feel supernumerary. Example 3, a seascape for band, illuminates the point. The opening strands are three-fold: in the upper parts, a rising figure makes reference to an evocative shanty; nearer the centre, quaver movement suggests the swell of the sea; in the bass, sustained two-octave pedal points give a feeling of immense depth. Each linear strand has some interest and adumbrates music to come. The tendency at the beginning of a piece when all the parts come together, is to clog the texture. Strong, bold lines make for an effective gambit and as the instruments are for the most part well-matched dynamically, crescendi and diminuendi played by the whole band make a striking impact (see pages 124–5).

Unison and octave, used to thicken individual lines and counter-melodies or given to the entire band at the beginning or end of a piece, should not be overlooked:

Rondo from *Little Suite for Brass* (op. 80) by Malcolm Arnold

In contrapuntal (example 4), or canonic writing (example 5), each strand of the composition should be interwoven so as to be well-spaced from another and clearly distinguishable from its accompaniment, if the thread of continuity is to be preserved within the all-brass texture (see pages 126–8).

With a particularly beautiful folk song, it can be arresting to start straight in, treating it as an unaccompanied cornet or euphonium solo, with the rest of the band entering in verse two. Laying bare its musical line and phrase in this way serves to engage listeners' attention and retain it whilst the tune unfolds leaving them interested in what will happen next. This can be a very effective way of beginning after shrinking from obvious openings and despairing of unobvious ones – but the melody itself must be striking otherwise a dull arrangement will result. Concluding is more problematic; much will depend upon what has gone before but some form of recapitulation will usually occur. We may choose to end with a fadeout or alternatively, make the ending the climax of the arrangement. We may combine the opening melody with a contrasting one or choose to set it canonically. Subtle contrasts are the keynotes.

So far we have discussed tonal and textural contrast with specific regard to writing for young players. Contrast can be effected in other ways: namely, harmonically, rhythmically and stylistically. Quite naturally, in a monochrome, all-brass combination these means predominate.

With its strong, vocal quality the brass band is especially given to harmonic contrast. A harmonic progression may alter with each reappearance of a recurring phrase, or new harmonies can be put aside to be brought in as a *bonne-bouche* at the end. Joseph Horovitz has an unerring flair for subtle shifts of harmony. Following is an extract from his *Sinfonietta*, scored for brass band by Bram Gay. Nearing the end of the second movement this *cri de coeur* enters three times, the underlying sustaining harmonies intensifying to an expansive climax then resolving and dissolving away again:

Brass band players, like their wind band counterparts, are adept and versatile stylists. The foregoing example exploits the brass band's inherent legato capacity, but at the opposite extreme of the stylistic continuum – the strongly-accented *brillante* effects – the band is equally at ease. Fanfares may appear less thrilling than of old unless given a new slant; William Mathias, in *Vivat Regina*, does just that:

Example 3:

Fruits de Mer

124

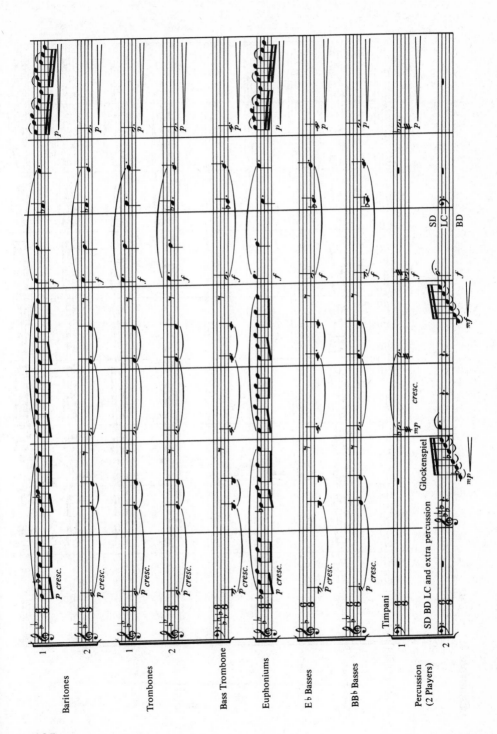

Example 4:

What Shall we do with the Drunken Sailor?

arr. K. Thompson

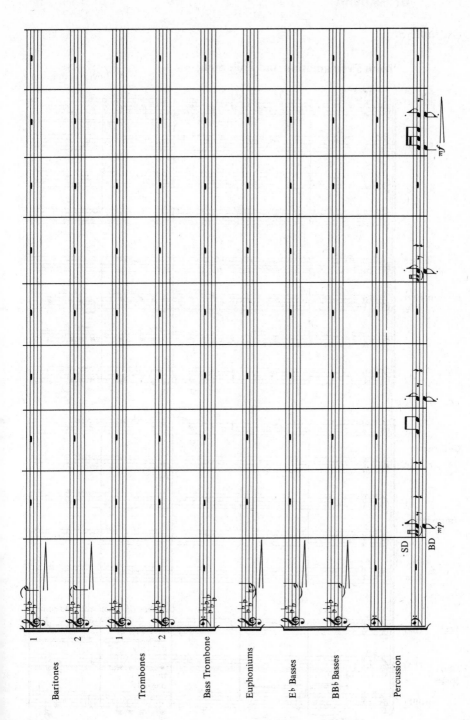

Example 5:

from Proclamation and Folk Song

Kevin Thompson

The arresting fanfare opening in Anthony Hedges setting of *Psalm 104*, is of an antiphonal and polytonal type. Nearing the end of the phrase he simultaneously combines chords of different tonal centres:

Malcolm Arnold too, makes martial effects sound fresh. Here are the opening bars of his first *Little Suite for Brass*. Resolute and rhythmically taut, this first movement, like the rest of the work, is a model of tonal and articulatory contrast within the brass band medium:

Leaving the high brass to sustain the final chord beyond that of the rest of the band, has almost become a cliché. A clever humorist, however, can turn a cliché back on itself. Here are the penultimate and final chords of *Saturday Market* by Anthony Hedges:

It is worth the reminder that the instruments are intrinsically capable of being played with greater agility than their orchestral equivalents: fast-moving semiquaver runs, trills, double and triple tonguing are part and parcel of any crack player's technique. For instance, the following passage, from an arrangement of 'What Shall we do With the Drunken Sailor', is, with practice, eminently playable by music centre players if ambitious for school band:

To say that the brass player's capability for quick, clearly-articulated tonguing has provided a source of stimulation for many a composition is only to acknowledge an obvious truth. Although the facility for rapid reiteration of the same note has been largely overworked, there are ways of using it which, though characteristic and far from new, remain exciting; deploying it to engender vigorous, energetic rhythmic motifs is one. *Count Down* by Paul Patterson has forceful recurring rhythm patterns, not untypical of music by this composer, himself a former trombonist (see pages 132–3).

Pyramids and cascades, quite simply ascending and descending broken chords whereby each player or group of players sustains a different note of the series, are as effective for the brass band as for any other ensemble. Resounding pyramids, built on perfect fifths, crisply and resourcefully round-off *A Traditional Hornpipe Suite* by Adrian Cruft:

Bell tone effects work well throughout the band but especially so with the cylindrical trombones, and arpeggiated figures played by the euphonium can give rhythmic impetus to an otherwise slow-moving harmonic passage (see example 2 on pages 118–19).

Another way of adding movement (as we see in the following extract from an arrangement of 'I'se the B'y that Builds the Boat' combined with 'Shenandoah') is to superimpose a faster, perhaps earlier, motif on a slower-moving one:

Count Down

Paul Patterson

Allegro con spirito (♩=120)

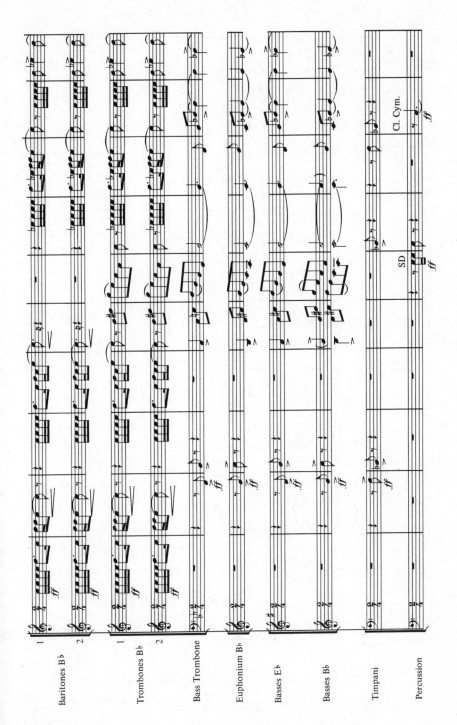

Example 6a: from Proclamation and Folk Song

Kevin Thompson

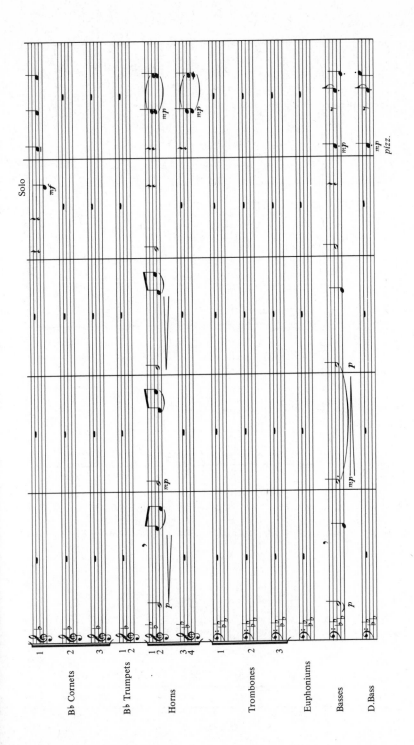

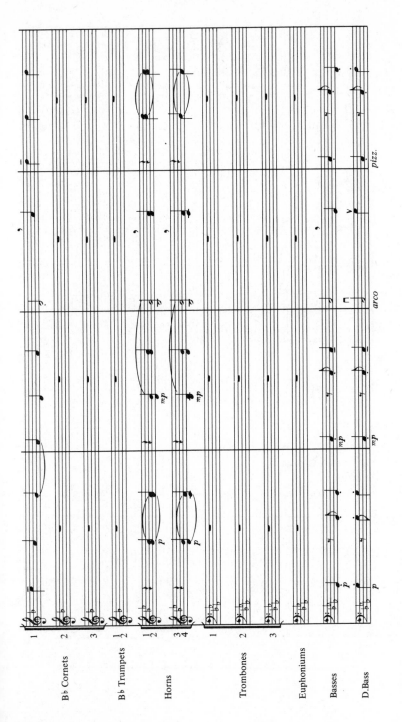

138

Example 6b:

from Proclamation and Folk Song

Kevin Thompson

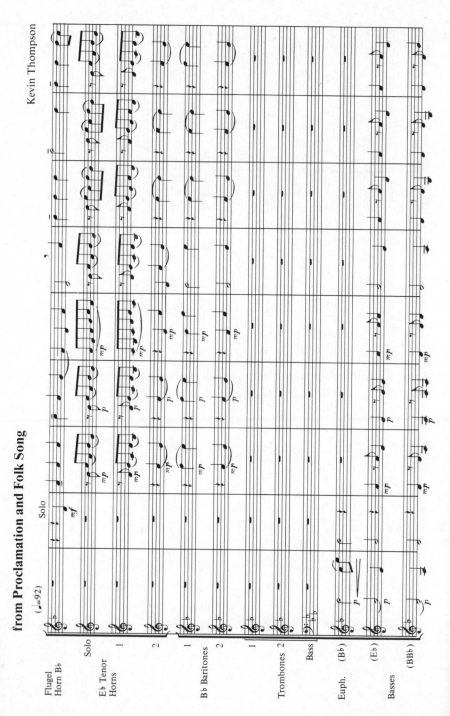

Transcribing from wind band to brass band and the reverse

In the wind band the degree of tonal separation is such that leading melodic lines can be easily and clearly heard. For the same lines to predominate in the brass band medium, pitch separation may assume prior importance as tonal contrast is less marked (see pages 134–8).

The melody in the wind band score (example 6a) is played by a single cornet player accompanied by flautists and clarinettists. The contrast of tonal quality between these throws melody and accompaniment into bold relief, so much so that we can afford to closely-place, and at times cross, the two linear strands. In the other setting, the brass band version (example 6b), the flugel takes the melody line accompanied by tenor horns. If we were to use the same voicings both melody and accompaniment would lack definition. The solution is relatively simple: unclutter and point up the melody line by keeping the accompaniment below it.

As already mentioned, whereas the wind band is heavy in the treble register the brass band is heavy in the tenor register. Neither has the fullness of the orchestra in its top range, though the wind band, with piccolo, E flat and B flat clarinets, is somewhat better placed than the brass band, which in the high register has the soprano cornet as its sole representative, and in any case cannot equal the pitch of piccolo, E flat clarinet or orchestral strings.

In this sense, when re-arranging from wind band to brass band, it is necessary to telescope the upper parts of the score. When transcribing from brass band to wind band, it is desirable to open out the upper voices. In both cases it is a question less of re-allocating the parts at a suitable pitch; more a matter of conceiving and re-working them, in the most imaginative and elegant scoring we can muster. That would seem a valid concept of what a transcription should be. It might involve replacing, say, a fast-tonguing passage, characteristic of cornets but not of clarinets, with equally characteristic high, woodwind trills to engender the same sense of excitement and achievement. Just as in speech, whilst the accent may be different, the message is much the same. Examples 7a and 7b show the same passage scored for wind band and brass band respectively (see pages 140–2).

It goes without saying that the two instrumentations correspond neither tonally nor, in some cases, pitchwise; they are at best approximate counterparts. The important thing is to ensure that a score is well-crafted in terms of the instrumental forces available, their overall compass, tonal and dynamic range. The following table itemises wind band

Example 7a:

from Proclamation and Folk Song

Kevin Thompson

141

Example 7b:

from Proclamation and Folk Song

Kevin Thompson

and brass band 'equivalents'. It should, it is emphasised, be taken only as a rough guide:

Wind Band	Brass Band
flutes	
piccolo	soprano cornet (at a comfortable pitch)
E flat clarinet	
oboes	solo cornet or soprano cornet
B flat clarinets	cornets, flugel, or tenor horns (for the low register of the clarinet)
E flat alto clarinet	tenor horns
B flat bass clarinet	euphoniums, baritones, trombones, or basses
bassoons	
alto saxophones	tenor horns, or flugel (if in the high register of the alto sax)
tenor saxophone	euphonium or baritone
baritone saxophone	E flat bass
cornets	cornets
trumpets	
French horns	flugel and tenor horns
trombones	trombones
euphoniums	euphoniums, baritones
tubas	basses
double bass	
timpani	timpani
percussion	percussion

15 Brass band repertoire: *quo vadis?*

In 1930 Peter Warlock wrote:

> English choral music has vastly improved during the last thirty years, but
> the quality of the average brass-band programme leaves much to be
> desired. No musical combination is so badly in need of original compo-
> sitions and of artistically-scored arrangements of other good music. At
> present there is a lamentable lack of enterprise on the part of our pub-
> lishers; operatic pot-pourris and showy Victorian cornet solos still pre-
> dominate in their brass-band catalogues, and several firms, as I know
> from personal experience, will not consider brass-band publications at
> all, being apparently as unaware as Grove's Dictionary of the growing
> appetite for such music (*Daily Telegraph*, 17 September 1930).

At the time, the operatic pot-pourris and the showy Victorian cornet
solos Warlock mentioned, were interspersed with abridged transcriptions of overtures, extracts from symphonies, lengthy romantic tone-
poems, waltzes and quick-step marches, all of which provided grist for
the mill of town and village brass bands.

But how different is it today? Even the most perfunctory glance
shows that it is substantially different. Of the once familiar mixture, the
waltzes and the operatic selections have all but disappeared; kitsch Victorian *air-varies*, transcripted overtures, symphonies and tone poems
are becoming more and more things of the past, though they have not
quite ossified as yet. But despite the relentless march of progress, the
indigenous quick-step march, whether regarded with a feeling of
nostalgia or a sense of nausea, marches on.

Intended not for use on the march but designed expressly for contesting, the quick-step march has a formalised *da capo* structure, the essential elements comprising: introduction, a brilliantly ornamented
exposition played by the solo cornet, an energetic, emphatically
articulated bass solo, and a contrasting lyrical trio in a related key. The
greater the contrast between the elements, the greater the effect.

Some bands have made particular marches their own by using them as
signature tunes. Rumour has it that at the outdoor, quick-step march
contests held in Saddleworth each Whit Friday, rival bandsmen arriving

to play have been known to give up their bid to wrest the cup after hearing in the distance the distinctive strains of *Knight Templar* (Allan), or *Queensbury* (Kaye), marches traditionally associated with Black Dyke. The story shows the sort of grudging admiration bandsmen have for the skill and the stylised way in which a rival band's own contest marches are played. Quick-step marches, however, make up only a part of the repertoire. What of the rest?

Once, especially during the early sixties and even as far as the seventies, when the repertoire seemed to reach something of an impasse, it looked as if the brass band were to be haunted by the spectre of its own demise:

> . . . a relic of the 'great' Britain of pre-1914 . . . little more than a sentimental memory, like steam-trains, fish-and-chips, comic postcards – a cloth cap joke in fact (A. Butterworth, *Music in Education*, 34, 342 (1970) pp. 152–3).

Fortunately, the demise did not come about. Indeed, a resurgence of the band's rôle as a 'purveyor' (as Butterworth calls it) of popular music is currently in play. True, the rise of entertainment contests and the success of televised competitions, Best of Brass and Granada Band of the Year, have leavened the traditional fare with 'easy-listening' pop and other lightweight pieces. Sentimentality, too, is as apparent today as ever. But alongside this development we have seen the emergence of a more substantial, enduring repertoire: a re-birth of serious brass band music.

Did this renaissance happen through leadership? Or did it happen through the welling-up of a new culture from below, and its adoption by publishers and the panjandrums of the brass band world? The answer, as always, is that it was a combination of all these things.

Thanks to vital seminal figures, in particular Elgar Howarth (Harrison Birtwistle's *Grimethorpe Aria* was to have an unprecedented effect on the brass band repertory), the brass band's gallant attempt to catch up with the twentieth century and overcome some of its insular indifference to other forms of music, bodes well for the future. The 'cultural movement' – if it is not too pretentious to call it that – has tended to stem from two distinct yet interrelated sources: from professional players with experience of the orchestral and the larger music world returning to brass banding as conductors – and judging by the numbers doing so, it must be more than sentimental yearning that draws them back; and from composers – often situated in one of the groves of academe – involved with brass bands and working with them in a new way: people such as Edward Gregson and Derek Bourgeois. It may be questionable whether the views of these people reflect popular attitudes or those of a small sophisticated audience, but they appear to have taken the decision – intuitively, perhaps – that rather than kowtow to popular demand, they should try to influence that demand.

On the whole the music of composers such as Gregson and Bourgeois has not been a total departure in terms of sound and sign, but sufficiently different for bandsmen to reflect on it, try to relate it to what they already know, and perhaps ultimately to re-think their assumptions about twentieth-century music.

This propensity of players to reflect on the composer's motives is especially true of bandsmen who are well used to programmatic pieces. It is something akin to a Rorschach inkblot test, only bandsmen project their fantasies onto the music. This fondness for music which tells a story, illustrates a scene, or portrays an event stems back to the origins of the movement when works were based on the eternal themes: love, death, toil and poverty. Indeed, the programme implicit in the title of the first original test-piece, Percy Fletcher's *Labour and Love* commissioned by John Henry Iles for the National Championship of 1913 made an ideal subject for brass band dramatisation.

So the bandsmen's legendary wariness of new music could not have been breached other than by degrees. The social strata were such that a chasm between the people who wrote the music and those who played it would have been easy to imagine. But though the bandsmen's image of being conservative and unreceptive to new ideas may still be true enough, there is a substantial body of opinion that sees it as imperative to keep up to date with the literature of today. It believes brass band music – like any other kind – must be alive, not of the archive, and that its composers should be allowed to dare, to venture, to experiment.

For many of the older brass band conductors the music of today has simply not been germane to their lives. In many particulars they may be desperately lacking in an appreciation of the wider music world outside of the brass band and especially twentieth-century compositional trends and influences. They know not what they are missing. But we should not set out to reproach anyone, least of all conductors. Today's brass band, after all, has come and is still coming to terms with the sounds of its own time. It is only by exposing its players and listeners to pieces that they would not have originally sought out for themselves that horizons will be expanded.

It is not, however, simply a matter of including a token contemporary piece in a traditional concert programme. That does not really address itself to the problem. There is, indeed, a sense in which to make simply passing reference to modern serious music in a traditional brass band programme can actually be a negative act, because it seems to relegate it to some sort of minor or inconsequential status. Introducing contemporary music has to be done in such a way as to show that it is well worth considering. Conductors and players have to be well-versed in the available literature and take into account the venue and the likely audience. Nowadays brass bands play at prestigious venues but seem all too often to let down both themselves and the movement as a whole by dispensing a programme more suited to park-bench listeners who perhaps chance to take in a piece or two with their mid-day fare than to seasoned, discerning concert-goers. Choosing a programme requires positive selection on the grounds of suitability bearing in mind that there is a growing audience for the new and the unfamiliar.

A substantial proportion of the new and unfamiliar has been commissioned for contests. Some, though specifically intended as contest pieces, are of unimpeachable musical quality and have become the classics of the brass band repertoire; others, with inspired moments, draw on a wide range of musically interesting generic material but are too infrequently heard; and still more, largely abject pastiche with little, if any, sense of permanency, radiate seemingly perennial appeal.

Contests pose something of a dilemma. The standard of brass bands in our country is due in large measure to the tradition of contesting and is such that today there are many performers with formidable techniques. Artistry and taste, however, are sometimes in short supply.

By and large the commissioning of major contest pieces has not so much launched relatively unknown composers from within the movement as endorsed already established composers writing for the medium. One publishing house, R. Smith, has stood since the twenties and early thirties as the cynosure of original contest repertoire. Composers who were taken on joined the elect – Elgar, Holst, Ireland, Bliss, Bantock and Howells – in the pantheon of twentieth-century brass band literature.

The publishing of brass band music is still a cottage industry. Many scores and parts look, even if they do not actually sound, home produced. The number of small self-publishing enterprises shows that, given access to photocopying and comb-bind facilities, practically anyone can set up in business. Would that business acumen took second place to musical ambitions.

The old, established publishers continue to pick their way over seventy years of original compositions, as well as fulfil a demand for all kinds of music, of which the shelf-life of some should have expired long ago. From time to time an adventurous publisher brings out a work that dares the expectations of the average bandsman – but so often in publishing successful innovation leads to cloning. The pleasure then for players and audiences alike is purely one of repetition. In the crowded field of brass band music, it is important to sort the wheat from the tares, for it is only the wheat that is nourishing and wholesome. For players who give up many hours sating their passion for the medium nothing less will do. It is, and it will remain, a labour of love.

The catalogues of two north of England publishers, one, the Manchester publishing house of Forsyth, the other, a Sheffield-based firm Hallamshire, have each issued publications serviceable for school bands and brass ensembles, the former publisher setting out deliberately to do so and having appreciably more impact, the latter almost incidentally.

Edited by Ifor James, 'Bandkraft' (Forsyth), is crafted to the requirements of incomplete bands. That the three albums which comprise the series are well thought-out is exemplified not only in that they come complete with both full scores and two-stave piano reductions, but also in the use of shareable, 'co-ordinated' parts: that is two parts printed together so that in addition to players having their own parts in front of them, they have those of others. This is a simple, effective idea, in which the advantages would seem to be three-fold: to allow players to cue-in vital passages that otherwise would be missing; to facilitate the inexperienced to pair-up with more advanced players; and to enable each player to know a little more of the music than his or her own single line part. Items run the gamut of styles and idioms – everything from a Passacaglia to Joplinesque – reflecting the series' contributors who rank amongst their number Gordon Jacob, Roy Newsome, John Golland, who wrote the title piece *Bandkraft*, and Harry Mortimer who advised.

The Hallamshire catalogue comprises for the most part overtly popular music though there are some classical arrangements. For schools, by far the most useful aspect of the publications is that many of them are arranged for three compatible instrumentations: brass band, wind band, and ten-piece – much of which was arranged for the James Shepherd Versatile Brass. The publisher did not foresee a market in schools for these ten-piece scorings, comprising: four cornets, tenor horn, trombone, bass trombone, euphonium, E flat bass and percussion.

The Hinrichsen First Band Book, which is, as its title suggests, the primer of a series, has far from run its course. Generations of beginners have cut their playing teeth on music from this tutor before moving on to other pieces when they have shown they can at least cope with the basics of the instruments. Encompassing a wide variety of folk songs, carols and brief excerpts from the classics, all the material is scored in four basic parts so that it is playable by a quartet coming together for the first time, or by a larger, established ensemble. Included in the score are teacher's notes, which are especially helpful to non-specialists, and two-stave piano reductions for rehearsal; a bold step as the projected tutor book was envisaged during the days when high pitched brass instruments predominated. Still, the two-stave reduction did allow the teacher to see at a glance the harmonic progressions of the pieces being rehearsed.

Published in the fifties in conjunction with the NSBBA under the editorship of the eclectic Kenneth Cook, the *Hinrichsen Brass Band Journal* was to set a precedent in the issuing of material specifically intended for school and educationally-based bands. Evolved from the practical situations encountered by the contributors teaching would-be brass players, the journal has a clear and positive sense of direction. The editorial panel – Eric Ball, Philip Catelinet and Denis Wright were amongst its number – conceived it to fulfil an urgent demand. Its rationale was to provide effective, musically satisfying pieces yet with minimal technical difficulties to meet the needs of school band players. The keys to its success were a willingness of the contributors to submit to a whole set of new criteria, clearly printed copies, and careful gradation of the series. In the primer especially, the gradients are sufficiently slight for the majority of students to take them in their stride.

Until recently, however, with young players making inroads into the available supply of intermediate standard literature, it became clear that an impasse, after an almost too easy start, was apparent. Another eclectic, Stuart Johnson, more prolific than any other individual writer of repertoire for school band, has eased the situation. Indeed his output has been substantial in a wider field of educational brass band music.

Young players find his *Four Dances for Brass* (Reakes), comprising blues, waltz, tango and ragtime, appealingly foot-tapping. The pieces fulfil the composer's avowed intention of familiarising would-be band members with some of the rhythmic patterns they will undoubtedly encounter sooner or later. In the same edition is the composer's *Hollyhedge March*; a pineapple pot-pourri, *Music from the Theatre of Mr. D'Oyly Carte*; and a graphic *Old Castle Suite*, scored for small band: soprano cornet, first and second cornets, two horns, baritone or trombone, two bass clef parts, euphonium or B flat bass, E flat bass and percussion. The music can be played by any combination from quartet to full band.

His contributions to the Hinrichsen series, the *Second* and *Third Band Books*, following in the footsteps of Kenneth Cook, are useful additions and abundant wells from which to draw. The second book comprises four each of originals and arrangements in four basic parts; the third book, a miscellany of six pieces in seven basic parts. Being of a moderately easy standard of difficulty, they are suitable for most bands of between two and three years' experience, as are his *Inter-*

mediate and *Second Intermediate Band Books* (R. Smith), with which they suggest comparison. Again, each of the intermediate books is a rich source of programme material.

Tutor books designed with the initial stages of learning in mind imply short pieces. Such is the case with Stuart Johnson's *Preliminary Band Book* (R. Smith), though the brevity and simplicity of the pieces leaves it a prey to criticisms – levelled by learners more advanced in age – of puerility. At some of the pieces chosen older 'Jack and Jills' may well baulk but at least younger players know them.

After a secure grounding in basic four-part ensemble playing, Stuart Johnson's *Progressive Band Book* (R. Smith), provides a springboard to full complement, intermediate pieces. Flexibly arranged, the pieces can be played by small ensembles provided that there is a minimum of eight players: two each of cornets, horns, tenor instruments (baritones or trombones), euphonium, B flat or E flat bass. They may also be used, as Johnson points out, by school brass bands of a more advanced standard to help new recruits to find their feet within the full band or, suitably transposed, by orchestral brass. The tutor ranges engagingly from sea shanties, through variations, a chorale prelude and a march, to Savoy and Schubert suites; programme items of a type harking back to the oldest popular repertoire – indeed in the introduction Johnson makes passing reference to alfresco performances.

Other music from the pen of the prolific Mr Johnson includes: *Two Pieces for Young Band*, comprising *A London Prelude*, and *A Children's March*; *A Northumbrian Suite*; *Kaleidoscope*; *A Circus Suite*, the 1980 test-piece for the Butlin's Youth final; *A March Overture*; a pop cantata for sopranos, altos and brass band *David and Goliath* (all published by R. Smith); *Festival Suite* (Hinrichsen); *Ceramic City Festival*; and a four-movement suite of miniatures, *Contrasts in Brass* (both Molenaar).

Patrick Rivers, who has acquired a solid reputation in the field of school brass band music, has arranged for young or inexperienced players several classics. These pieces can be found in the *Hinrichsen Brass Band Journal*, and in an old but still valuable collection, published by Bosworth in the late sixties, aptly titled *Pieces from the Classics*. Designed for school band members with one or maybe two years' playing experience, the arrangements – in five-part harmony – can be played by full band or with as few as five players, provided, that is, the quintet is a balanced one. The arranger's *Novello Band Book* is well-known, as are two originals: *Portrait of Brunel* (Studio), and *Rhapsody, Sons of the Waves* (Hinrichsen). Both pieces have been received with considerable enthusiasm over the years. A more recent piece, *Royal Parade March* (Reakes), is easy enough for all but the most elementary players.

Scored for four- and five-part ensemble with alternative transposed parts available, the series 'Junior Just Brass' (Chester), is essentially a collection of miniatures. Conventional in its unconventionality, to describe the collection merely as wide ranging is to do it a disservice. It is a rich assortment of scores. Represented are musics as diverse as Latin American dances, bluesy pop numbers, folk tunes, carols and contemporary originals. The scores allow for some approximations in instrumentation. However, not knowing the precise instrumental line-up of the given ensemble playing the pieces (which might be a mixture of orchestral and brass band transposing instruments), the publisher had little alternative but to issue the scores in C. This may hinder rather than help some teachers. Several of the pieces are of a musical aperitif type so for those with more contemporary, acquired tastes, *Just Brass*, without the qualifier 'junior', will prove even more tempting.

Edited and arranged by Denis Wright, the series 'Music for Brass Ensemble' (Novello) (to be precise, brass band ensemble as distinct from orchestral) has seen considerable mileage. Familiar and not so familiar pieces ripe for brass band transcription make up each of the three books. For the most part the collection remains firmly rooted in the seventeenth and eighteenth centuries; a select choice – as to be expected of the editor – but then these are books for those who enjoy a well-turned phrase more than the oft-turned page.

Staying with classic series, 'Music for Brass Players' (Universal Edition), edited and arranged by Rodney Mayes, is another choice collection with all the rarefied air of the concert hall and ill-fitting the bandstand. Whether or not the series sells, its aims are admirable: to provide music for small or incomplete brass ensembles up to full complement. Treble and bass clef editions are available for euphonium downwards, including a useful bass trombone part in treble clef with cues suitably placed for the tenor trombone's compass. Soprano and trombones are optional as are the basses since the euphonium sustains the bass line throughout. All the pieces have been culled only from monuments of the baroque, classical and romantic periods. But they are, when all's said and done – though it is perhaps an aloof churl who scoffs at the idea – transcriptions.

In a lighter vein, the series 'Twin Sets' (Fortune) is aimed specifically at school bands. Pairing pieces, the originators of this novel idea have included within the series novelty, rhythmic and tonal numbers, descriptive pieces, polkas, classics, solos and choral (*sic*) preludes. It seems the publisher has a penchant for job lots as the catalogue runs to four each of carols, marches, waltzes and folk tunes; a *School Album*, all without full scores; and dedicated to the Neston Youth Band, a *Triple Concerto for Cornet or Recorder, Bicycle Pump and Bell*.

Another enterprising collection, 'The Stateside Series' by Edrich Siebert (Studio Music) – the title gives just a hint of what is in store – is so designed as to be playable by an octet: two cornets, two horns, euphonium, trombone, bass and drums. Written within the safe range of elementary brass instrumentalists, the uppermost part extends no higher than D fourth line treble clef. Stars and stripes run, by way of the *Grand Canyon Galop* and the *Santa Fé Trail*, alphabetically from *Blue Grass Blues* and *Boston Bounce*, to *Texas Tango* and *Vermont* (a march).

Edrich Siebert and others contributed to *Eight Easy Band Marches* (Boosey & Hawkes), an anthology which came of age in 1982. Still a worthy introduction to the military march (as distinct from the brass band quick-step variety) it can be played by all-brass bands, wind bands, or a combination of the two.

Commissioned by the NSBA for one of its annual festivals *Praeludium* by Philip Lane (Paxton) was first performed in 1975 by the Redbridge Music School Band. It is then of music centre band level; perhaps a shade ambitious for the average school band. The instrumentation includes alternative parts for orchestral brass. Whilst the piece does not make excessive demands on technique, it is metrically more intricate than the norm: five and three time alternate almost measure by measure. An exposed unaccompanied passage where solo cornet and euphonium play in canon may worry all but the most consistent players. Nevertheless, it is a fresh rhythmically infectious piece.

The same may be said of Paul Patterson's piece *Count Down* (see pages 132–3), which is an immediately accessible, exciting work. After a racy start, rousing recurring rhythm patterns, requiring great crispness of attack, give way to a contrasting lyrical section before the piece is reanimated with relentless rhythmic drive. Written for the final of the Butlin's Youth Championship in 1975, the piece is within the grasp of a competent school band.

Two other advanced works (decidedly county youth band material) by the same composer – savant in contemporary ingenuities – are: *Chromascope* (1974) which is unusual in that at one point it requires of performers breathing sounds produced by them blowing through their mouthpieces; and *Cataclysm* (1975), as its title suggests a sudden and violent change – at least in the brass band world. Commissioned by the National Youth Brass Band, which gave the première under Marcus Dods, this seminal piece makes use of indeterminate notations so performers have, of necessity, to take a conscious, collaborative role in the process of making the music happen. *Count Down*, *Chromascope* and *Cataclysm* are all published by Weinberger.

Since one NYBB commission has been mentioned, it is perhaps an appropriate juncture at which to bring in another, *The Tableaux of the Heraldic Animals* (Novello hire library), by Richard Steinitz. An immense technical challenge – the title alone is one with which to conjure – this imaginative and colourful work was given its first performance at the Harrogate Festival of 1976 by the NYBB conducted by Arthur Butterworth, at that time Musical Adviser to the band.

Arthur Butterworth himself has contributed a number of programmatic, illustrative compositions for youth band. His *A Dales Suite* (Hinrichsen), written in 1964 for Ermysted's Grammar School Band in Skipton, has, incidentally, been re-scored for orchestra, rather in the manner Gordon Jacob transcribed Holst's *A Moorside Suite*, and Vaughan Williams' *Folk Song Suite*, works originally written for brass and military band respectively. Although the work was originally known as *An Embsay Suite*, its publisher suggested the adopted title as the more specific place name is little known outside of the immediate locality of the Yorkshire Dales. Subsequently, *Embsay* became the work's subtitle.

An excursion south resulted in *Blenheim* (R. Smith), a piece which, if use is made of the cued parts, can be performed with less than complete instrumentation. Described as a 'heroic' overture, it commemorates the Churchill family and was commissioned by another youth band, the Woodstock Band. Characteristically, the piece was first performed alfresco upon the steps of Blenheim Palace. But it is the northern landscape that remains a rich source of inspiration for this composer's tone-painting. The outdoor allusions, which are quite frank and deliberate, enhance his music's atmospheric, impressionistic quality.

The Path Across the Moors, originally composed in 1959 for orchestra – more commonly the case – was scored for brass band a decade later. Not intentionally youth band material, the piece was published as part of the 'Hinrichsen Brass Band Journal' so now if not indelibly associated with youth bands, it has acquired educational connotations; the soprano and timpani parts may be dispensed with if the cues are taken by other players. His *Winter Music* (MS) of 1982, portrays the passage from winter to spring. Again, though not strictly for youth band, it is intended for 'young' band.

The subject matter of the imaginative *Three Impressions for Brass* (Studio), is such that it could only truly be played by the musical medium chosen. It is this work that the composer himself regards as his finest within the genre, certainly it would seem to be his best known. Commissioned by the Northumberland County Youth Band in 1968, it was first performed at the Morpeth Festival of the same year. Asked to provide a work which might have local connections, the composer came across a book containing etchings and woodcuts of various industrial scenes and archaeological artefacts of nineteenth-century Northumberland. *Three Impressions* then, delineates scenes illustrated within the book: *Wylam Colliery (1839)*, an evocative scene of dark colliery workings, massive coal wagons, and the strain and effort of 'Puffing Billy'; and *Deserted Farm (1840)*, a forlorn worked-out small-holding, impoverished and beset by the growing encroachment of quarries and railways on a hitherto rural scene of eighteenth-century England – indeed, a remnant of another time. These two settings form the first and second movements respectively. The final movement – played countless times by all kinds of brass bands – is entitled *The Royal Border Bridge, Berwick-on-Tweed (1850)*, and is an evocation of George Stephenson's magnificent piece of railway engineering. Aligning itself as it does with such settings, the brass band is perhaps the most natural mode of musically presenting them.

Joseph Horovitz has a rare gift for light music. His *Sinfonietta* (Novello), an enchanting, clever work, was conceived for brass band in 1970 and re-scored for light orchestra in 1971. In its original form, scored by Bram Gay, the general editor of the publisher's brass band series, it lies well for competent youth band and makes rewarding study. The whole work is a gem.

Three pieces from the composer's delightful *Music Hall Suite* (Novello) of 1964, have been transcribed – again by Bram Gay – from brass quintet to brass band, so it hardly amounts to sacrilege, merely an abridgement. The three movements comprise *Soft-Shoe-Shuffle*, *Adagio-Team* and *'Les Girls'*. Like *Sinfonietta*, the suite has a most exciting finale.

Overture: Provence (Novello, 1969) by Bryan Kelly, is the first of several works the composer has written for brass band. It is performable with less than full band and wherever secondary parts are essential they are cued into the primary ones. Inspiration for the piece came after a particularly memorable holiday spent in the Provençal region of France. Although the work is joyous it is neither overtly folksy nor obviously Gallic – though the composer, like Joseph Horovitz, studied with Nadia Boulanger in Paris. *Provence* seems to embody the festal spirit of Southern France. Its sharply-accentuated Terpsichorean rhythms are similar in kind to those in a piece inspired by a different locale, the *Edinburgh Dances* (Novello). Composed for the NYBBS, this four-movement suite of dances was premièred in 1973 by its dedicatees in the city from whence it takes its title. Two more pieces by Bryan Kelly were conceived with youth bands in mind: they are *Divertimento*, an earlier work (1969) for the National Youth Brass Band of Scotland; and another piece which draws its title from the Mediterranean, *Andalucia*. The piece was commissioned for the finals of the Butlin's Youth Brass Band Championship in 1976. Both works are published by Novello.

Continuing the musical travelogue, his *March – Washington DC* (Novello) is light and bright. Its bracing mixture of punch and subtlety, its rag rhythms, and its dedication to 'friends in Washington DC', confirm it as something of a composite Anglo-American entente. Whilst not specifically intended for youth bands it is, nevertheless, within their range. A more recent work, *Partita* (Boosey and Hawkes), was chosen for the youth section qualifying contests in 1984.

Song of Freedom by Malcolm Arnold (Studio Music), for children's voices – a chorus of sopranos and altos – and brass band, was commissioned in 1970 by the NSB(B)A to commemorate its twenty-first anniversary in 1973. The idea was to bring into being a work for children's chorus and brass band within the scope of an average school band and choir. The first performance was given by the Netteswell School Band and Choir conducted by the composer. The text of the four-movement work draws on a number of poems by schoolchildren who responded to a competition on the subject of 'freedom'. His *Padstow Lifeboat* and two *Little Suites for Brass* (both Studio Music) (the first commissioned by the NYBBS in 1963, the second written in 1967 for the Cornwall Youth Band) are more widely known and loved.

Like Malcolm Arnold, Anthony Hedges writes music of the people. His is a style of expression that is easily assimilated, abounding as it does in singable tunes. In his brass band writing broad fanfare motifs contrast with busy melodic figures eminently suited to the medium. He has written several distinctive works for band including a setting of *Psalm 104* (Chappell), commissioned by York and District Brass Band Association, again for children's voices and brass band and first performed in 1973; a three-movement suite, written in 1976, *Prelude, Nocturne and March* (Westfield), alternately joyous, laid-back and processional; and an up-market *Saturday Market* (R. Smith), an overture embodying, with piercing vividness, all the bustle and commotion of Beverley Market Place, and a work selected for the Butlin's Youth Brass Band Championships in 1982.

The name Gordon Jacob engraved under the heading of a composition or arrangement is a near-universal imprimatur. If the composer had an affinity with wind instruments and a particular penchant for their textual colour, then his writing for all-brass combination was no less painstaking, intelligently balanced and of a consistently high calibre. His compositions and arrangements, distinguished by their clarity of texture, set a standard by which other writers are judged. The compositions display a disarmingly tonal idiom, well-suited to the brass band medium: the arrangements are so exquisitely well-wrought as to enhance the original. The quantity of brass band works that have emanated from behind the green baize door of the composer's study is considerable, so the following pieces are necessarily but a sample playable by youth bands.

His three-movement *Suite in B flat* (R. Smith), has become something of a standard. A wind band version of the same suite has recently been published. Both scorings have all the sensitivity and quality of craftsmanship we came to expect of the composer. The same hallmarks are present in the *Second Suite for Brass Band* (Molenaar), written for the National Youth Brass Band of Scotland, and in the sparkling and arresting *Fanfare and National Anthem* (Novello), though why the score and parts continue to be available only on hire remains a complete mystery.

The directness and economy of his style can be heard in the simple setting of *Sospan Fach* (the little saucepan). Subtitled 'A Prelude to a Welsh Football Match', the march lies well within the capabilities of an established school band; even more so do his *Two Chorale Preludes* on Melcombe and Abridge. Nearing the end of *A Victorian Rhapsody* (a fey collection of songs), the composer's skill as a contrapuntist is glimpsed. Wryly capturing the spirit of popular song and the ethos of an era, the impressions the work sets down are full of imagery, so clearly those of a sepia photograph (all Novello).

Octogenarian Eric Ball has won a very special respect from bandsmen, and within the movement his influence is unparalleled. In respect of brass band literature he looms large: the composer is indefatigable; his music, full of import for bandsmen the world over, is deeply sincere.

Just as in terms of wind band music Gordon Jacob was regarded as the doyen of British composers, Eric Ball may today be similarly considered in brass band music. Like his former confrère, he has continued to write into his eighties and he shares a similar uncommon knack for part-writing – knowing so well the characteristics of each instrument and pitching its part at the appropriate level for its exponent. His understanding and detailed knowledge of the collective instrumentation he writes for is such that much of his music is suitable for youth bands. Experienced players can, after all, cope with parts that lie uneasily for the instrument; beginners cannot. Further, his music is popular because it is reassuringly familiar and accessible. It is these facts which contribute to the respect his music has earned. It stands to reason then that youth bands should have claimed so many of his works for their own: the fantasy in four movements *Indian Summer*; the fantasia based on Swiss folktunes, *In Switzerland*, playable with as few as twelve players; *Three Songs Without Words*; *Petite Suite de Ballet* (all R. Smith); a three-movement suite commissioned for the 1971 youth finals, *English Country Scenes* (Novello); and three *Rhapsodies on Negro Spirituals* (each published by Boosey and Hawkes); these are but a few examples of a much larger repertoire of music by Eric Ball regularly dispensed by youth bands.

There are, of course, a sizeable number of works that have come to be regarded as virtually, if not exclusively, youth band property. Some works were envisaged as lower-section contest pieces; others were conceived with educationally-based bands in mind.

A national composers' competition for music suitable for school and youth brass bands took place in London in 1976. Organised by the National School Brass Band Association and sponsored by Dynatron, the competition attracted much attention. A distinguished panel of adjudicators including John Gardner, Edward Gregson and Joseph Horovitz, under the chairmanship of Sir Lennox Berkeley, chose the prizewinners – also the name which was to become the title of Philip Sparke's *Concert Overture – The Prizewinners*, and the winning entry. Other prizewinners were: *A Spring Overture* by Philip Lane (R. Smith), runner-up; with *Rhapsodic Prelude* by David Lyon (MS) – the composer has recently revised the work extensively – and *Overture to Youth* by Eric Hughes (Studio), taking third and fourth places respectively.

The Prizewinners (R. Smith) has since become a much played item by youth and adult bands alike, and deservedly so. It is rivalled in popularity only by the same composer's *Concert Prelude* (R. Smith) which makes for a splendid curtain raiser. With more than the occasional stylish, well-turned phrase, the work – set as the test-piece for the 1977 Butlin's Youth Championships – shows the composer's capacity to write attractive, uncomplicated music. Philip Sparke's *A Tameside Overture* (R. Smith), within the same genre of light concert openers, is a more recent accession to the repertoire. The piece was commissioned by Yorkshire Bank for a week-long brass course organised by Tameside in 1982.

The charm of such pieces lies partly in that they engage the listeners' attention within the first few minutes, and partly in the fact that they provide an alternative to traditional opening fare – the quick-step march. Many of these preludes (concert overtures, opening numbers, however they are termed) have a similar shape: a shape which comes in several recognisable guises. They fuse two or more strands of composition though there are, of course (lest the impression should be given of there being a one-size pret-à-porter collection), some works which do not readily conform either wholly or in part to the following generalisation. Briefly, their general structure consists of a fanfare, or march-like introductory motif followed by a quick-moving first subject, a contrasting more augmented second subject, some development rounded off either by a return to the opening idea, or a broad restatement pointing-up one of the two main subjects.

Few have marshalled these effects more strikingly than Edward Gregson who with *March Prelude* (Novello), written in 1968, was able to steal a march on others. Though an early, compact work it is nevertheless quite in character, relatively seamless, and despite its brevity shows considerable style and development. That it is written within the limited range of school band players – the composer was, incidentally, the youngest ever to write for the Championship Section of the National Finals – is no less remarkable. Cast in a similar mould is his stirring *Prelude for an Occasion* (R. Smith) of 1970, now firmly a staple of youth and adult bands alike.

The music of Edward Gregson has come to be regarded not as mere contemporary contest-fodder, but as an intensely rewarding cornerstone of the modern repertoire. A vernacular composer, his musical language, though of an abstract character, was from the outset that of the brass band. By and large it did not alienate the older band fraternity. Without backtracking into the past it was accessible, yet it took a sufficiently progressive step to satisfy discerning contemporary denizens of bandrooms. It was in all essentials what the brass band world was looking for – if it were looking at all. His music picked a delicate path of indelicacy between the previous Vinters and the contemporary Pattersons of the repertoire. Of course, on occasion the same path had been chosen before but no one had taken it so wholeheartedly nor so intelligently.

To date three of his works have been commissioned by youth bands (each subsequently published by R. Smith). Two were commissioned by the Redbridge Youth Band, the first, *Partita* in 1971 – comprising *Intrada*, *Chorale* and *Variations*, *March* – is based on the thirteenth-century plainsong *Dies Irae*; the second *Intrada* in 1972; and, within the same year, a third, *Concerto Grosso*, for cornet, horn, euphonium, trombone soloists and brass band, which was commissioned by the National Youth Brass Band of Scotland.

Other music suitably placed for youth bands includes his: three-movement suite *Voices of Youth*, *Patterns*, *A Swedish March* (all R.Smith); *New Horizons for Beginner Brass Ensemble* (Belwin Mills), a tutor for five-part variable instrumentation; and though not intended as 'educational' music, *Music for Greenwich* (Boosey and Hawkes). Commissioned in 1980 for the London production of Peter Buckman's play 'All Together Now', the piece is playable by bands of less than full complement. Cued into other parts, soprano and bass trombone are optional; the ripieno cornet part has been omitted altogether.

Finally, the omission here of several other works, many of which are at least county youth band standard, would be woeful. This repertoire then, is of a kind that school players might eventually aspire to.

Mention should be made of five more NYBBS commissions: Alan Rawsthorne's only work for brass band, and one which is rife with difficulties, *Suite for Brass Band* (OUP, hire only) written in 1964; Martin Dalby's *Music for Brass Band* (Boosey & Hawkes, hire library) written the following year: in 1966 *Variations for Brass Band* by Thea Musgrave (Chester); in 1967 *Sinfonietta* by Thomas Wilson (R. Smith); and in 1968 *The Battle of St. John's Town* by Cedric Thorpe Davie (Scotus).

A triptych of pieces by Gareth Wood ought to be included: *Coliseum* written for the final of the 1977 Butlin's Youth Championship; a tone-poem entitled *Culloden Moor*, descriptive of the Battle of Culloden and commissioned by the NYBBS in 1978; and *The Margam Stones*, a suite of three movements commissioned by the West Glamorgan Youth Brass Band in 1979 and chosen as the test-piece for the 1981 youth final (all R. Smith).

Altitude by George Benjamin (Faber), winner of the young composers' competition organised by the NSBBA in 1978 for which over eighty scores were submitted, displays a maturity which is almost inconceivable in someone so young – the composer was at the time of the competition still a pupil at Westminster School.

Account should also be taken of the following: two works by Derek Bourgeois – *Aspirations*, written as the test-piece for the 1983 youth final, and, for the Redbridge Youth Band, *Concerto for Brass Quintet and Band* (both R. Smith); two by Roy Slack – *Alacita* (Hinrichsen), written in 1968 for the Barnet Schools' Brass Band, and *Fanfare for a Festival* (Paul Publications, 1983), dedicated to the Newham Academy Youth Band; two more commissioned for the youth finals of 1978 and 1979 respectively, Gordon Langford's *Overture: Metropolis* (Chandos), and Philip Catelinet's *Three Sketches for Brass Band* (Novello); and two by Roy Newsome, *Restormel Castle* (Fortune), composed in 1972 for the Cornwall Youth Brass Band, and *Westwood Suite* (Studio), for the Oldham Music Centre Band in 1984.

Last but not least are two marches, both titled with an acronym as is something of a tradition: one, written in 1968 by Bryden Thomson, *The NYBBS* (Chandos) – the commissioner is obvious; and another, the *Three B's* (MS), again written by Roy Newsome in recognition of the fortieth anniversary in 1983 of Besses Boy's Band. Reflected in the first main theme, which is based on a reiteration of three b's, the same sobriquet might equally have been derived from the senior band Besses o' th' Barn; one of the bands from which it all started in 1853.

Select bibliography

Arrand, D. 'It Couldn't Happen Here', *British Mouthpiece*, 31 January 1981

Bainbridge, C. *Brass Triumphant*, London: Frederick Muller Ltd, 1980

Band Music Guide, 7th edn, Illinois: The Instrumental Co. (undated)

Bashford, R. 'The Royal Military School of Music, *Music Teacher*, vol. 59, no. 8, 1980

Bennett, R.R. *Instrumentally Speaking*, Melville, NY: Belwin Mills, 1975

Bradbury, F.H. (ed.) *Directory of British Brass Bands*, York: British Federation of Brass Bands, 1981

Brand, G. *Training the School Brass Band*, National School Band Association, Brass Brochures 5, 1977

Brand, V. & G. (eds.) *Brass Bands in the 20th Century*, Letchworth, Herts: Egon Publishers, 1979

Brooks, A. 'Marching Bands', *The Times Educational Supplement*, 21 April 1978

Butterworth, A. 'The Brass Band – A Cloth Cap Joke?', *Music in Education*, vol. 34, no. 342, 1970; vol. 34, no. 343, 1970

Cacavas, J. *Music Arranging and Orchestration*, Melville, NY: Belwin Mills, 1975

Carlton, M. 'Repertory: Wind Band', *Music in Education*, vol. 42, no. 391, 1978

Carse, A. *Musical Wind Instruments*, London: Macmillan, 1939

Cipolla, F.J. and Camus, R.F. *Oom Pah Pah: The Great American Band*, Exhibition catalogue, New York, Dallas and Milwaukee, 1982–3

Constitution of the National School Band Association, Summer 1980

Cook, K. (compiler) *'Oh, Listen to the Band'*, London: Hinrichsen, 1950

Cook, K. and Caisley, L. *Music Through the Brass Band*, London; Hinrichsen, 1953

Cooper, T.L. *Brass Bands of Yorkshire*, Clapham, Yorkshire: Dalesman Publishing, 1974

Davies, R.L. 'Music Through the Band', *Music Teacher*, vol. 51, no. 12, 1972; vol. 52, no. 1, 1973

DeYoung, D. 'Music Literature for Band and Wind Ensembles', *Music Educators Journal*, December 1977

Dillon, S. 'The Concert Band in School and Music Centre', *Music in Education*, vol. 42, no. 399, 1978

Draper, F.C. 'The Development of Brass Wind Instruments' in F. Wright (ed.) *Brass Today*, London: Besson, 1954

Dumesil, R. 'Le Conservatoire de Paris', unpublished paper, Paris Conservatoire, 1983

Edsall, T. 'Our Side of the Tracks', *Ozoompah!* 45, August 1983 (Australian Brass Bands Association)

Edwards, L.W. and Katterjohn, A.D. 'Instilling Lasting Musical and Aesthetic Values in High School Band Members', *Music Educators Journal*, January 1976

Emerson, G. *More Ideas for Wind Orchestras*, Ampleforth, Yorks: Emerson Edition, 1975

Everett, T.G. 'It's Easier Than you Think – Commissioning Music for High School Band', *Music Educators Journal*, January 1976

Farmer, H.G. *The Rise and Development of Military Music* (reprinted 1970), New York: Books for Libraries Press, 1912

Fennell, F. *Time and the Winds: A Short History of the Use of Wind Instruments in the Orchestra, Band and the Wind Ensemble*, Kenosha, Wisconsin: Leblanc, 1954

Gammond, P. and Horricks, R. *Brass Bands*, Cambridge: Patrick Stephens, 1980

Garofalo, R. 'A New Plan for Concert Band', *Music Educators Journal*, April 1981

'A Study Guide for Teaching the History of Western Music in Secondary School Band Class' (a review of D.S. Goedecke, unpublished Ph.D. thesis), *Council for Research in Music Education, Bulletin*, no. 56, Fall 1978

'An Evaluation of Compositions for Wind Band According to Specific Criteria of Serious Artistic Merit' (a review of A.E. Ostling, unpublished Ph.D. thesis, University of Iowa, 1978), *Council for Research in Music Education Bulletin*, no. 64, Fall 1980

Garofalo, R. and Whaley, G. 'The Symphonic Wind Ensemble: Seating for Sound Improvement', *Music Educators Journal*, May 1976

Gay, B. 'The Brass Band: What Now?', *Music in Education*, vol. 34, no. 344, 1970

'New Music for the Brass Band', *Music in Education*, vol. 34, no. 341, 1970

Goldman, R.F. *The Band's Music*, New York: Pitman, 1938

The Wind Band, Boston: Allyn and Bacon, 1961

Graham, A.P. *Great Bands of America*, New York: Nelson, 1951

Hellyer, R. 'Harmoniemusik' in S. Sadie (ed.), *The New Grove Dictionary of Music and Musicians*, vol. 8, London: Macmillan, 1981

Hind, H. *The Brass Band* (2nd edn), London: Boosey & Hawkes, 1952

'School Brass Bands', *Music in Education*, vol. 20, nos. 236, 237, 238, 239

Holvik, K.M. and Whitwell, D. 'The Emergence of a New Literature', *Music Educators Journal*, January 1976

Hullah Brown, J. *Instrumental Music in Schools*, London: Pitman, 1938

ILEA. *Instrumental Teaching*, London: ILEA, 1972

Jacob, G. *The Composer and his Art*, London: OUP, 1955

Orchestral Technique (3rd edn), London: OUP, 1982

Labuta, J.A. 'The Band as a Learning Laboratory', *Music Educators Journal*, January 1976

Lang, P.J. *Scoring for Band*, Melville, NY: Belwin Mills, 1950

Lawrence, I. *Brass in Your School*, London: OUP, 1975

    Composers and the Nature of Music Education, London: Scolar Press, 1978

Lawton, S.M. 'Wind Ensembles and Symphonic Wind Orchestras in Secondary Schools', in B. Rainbow (ed.), *Handbook for Music Teachers*, London: Novello, 1968

Light, P. 'Starting and Developing a Wind Band', *Music in Education*, vol. 42, March 1978

Lord, T. *The Brass Band in the Primary School*, National School Band Association, Brass Brochures 3 (undated)

Loukes, D. 'Music Goes to War', *Sounding Brass*, vol. 9, no. 4, Winter 1980

McCabe, D.W. *et al. The ASBDA Curriculum Guide: A Reference Book for School Band Directors*, Pittsburgh: Volkwein, 1973

McMurtary, M.J. *Group Music Making*, London: Longman, 1972

Machell, D. 'All Together Now, 1, 2, 3 . . . ', *Music Teacher*, vol. 59, no. 1, 1980

Marchand, D.J. 'A Design for Comprehensive Musicianship in the Senior High School Band Programme' (a review of R. Warner, unpublished Ph.D. Thesis), *Council for Research in Music Education Bulletin*, no. 52, Fall 1977

Morrison, R. 'Spare-time Brass Champions – or Professional Musicians?', *Classical Music*, 15 July 1978

Mortimer, H. *On Brass*, Sherborne, Dorset: Alphabooks, 1981

Nightingale, C.L. *The Teaching of Wind Instruments*, London: Novello, 1963

Oboussier, P. *Arranging Music for Young Players*, London: OUP, 1977

Peel, R. (ed.). *Journal of the British Association of Symphonic Bands and Wind Ensembles*, vol. 2, Spring 1983; Autumn 1983

Porter, M.M. *The Embouchure*, London: Boosey & Hawkes, 1967

Rees-Davies, B. (ed.). 'Woodwind and Brass in Schools', *Music Teacher*, vol. 52, no. 1, 1973

Renouf, D. (ed.). 'Band Musicianship Awards', *Music Teacher*, vol. 58, no. 1, 1979

Reynish, T. 'New Works for Wind Band', *Composer*, 79, Summer 1983

Reynolds, G. and Chatterley, A. *A Young Teacher's Guide to Class Music*, Borough Green, Kent: Novello, 1969

Reynolds, R. *et al. Wind Ensemble Literature* (2nd edn), Madison, Wisconsin: University of Wisconsin Bands, 1975

Rivers, P. *Arranging for Brass Band, Part 1 & 2*, National School Band Association, Brass Brochures 1 (undated)

Russell, J.F. and Elliott, J.H. *The Brass Band Movement*, London: Dent, 1936

Schools Council. *The Organisation of Small Group-Work in the Classroom*, Schools Council Project: Music in the Secondary School Curriculum, University of York, 1977

Siebert, E. *A Practical Guide to Instrumentation for the Brass Band*, London: Studio Music, 1976

Simms, J.R. 'How to Avoid a Headache', *Music in Education*, vol. 42, no. 391, 1978

Smith, N. and Stoutamire, A. *Band Music Notes*, San Diego, California: Kjos, 1977

Steadman-Allen, R. *Colour and Texture in the Brass Band Score*, London: Salvationist Publishing, 1980

Swanwick, K. 'The Parameters of Music Education', *Music Teacher*, vol. 57, no. 12, 1978

   'Teaching in Groups' (Education Supplement), *Classical Music*, 14 July 1979

Sweby, C. 'Brass Bands in Schools: Conclusion', *Music in Education*, vol. 34, no. 346, 1970

   'Music Through the Band', *Music Teacher*, vol. 51, no. 6, 1972; vol. 52, no. 2, 1973

Taylor, A. *Brass Bands*, London: Granada Publishing, 1979

   Labour and Love, London: Elm Tree, 1983

Taylor, D. *Music Now*, Milton Keynes: Open University Press, 1979

Thompson, K. 'Festival of Wind Instruments', *Music Teacher*, vol. 60, no. 2, 1981

   'Gordon Jacob', *The Instrumentalist*, vol. 38, no. 2, September 1983

   'Wind Band', *Music Teacher*, vol. 59, nos. 5 and 6, 1980

Trodd, G. 'Instrumental Music in British Education', *Music Teacher*, vol. 57, no. 10, 1978

Wagner, J. *Band Scoring*, New York: McGraw-Hill, 1960

Weerts, R. *Handbook of Rehearsal Techniques for the High School Band*, New York: Parker, 1976

   'Take Time', *Music Educators Journal*, January 1976

Weerts, R. (compiler). *Original Manuscript Music for Wind and Percussion Instruments*, Reston, Virginia: MENC Publications, 1973

Weir, C. *Village and Town Bands*, Aylesbury: Shire Publications, 1981

Whitwell, D. *A New History of Wind Music*, Evanston, Illinois: The Instrumentalist Company, 1972

Whitwell, D. and Ostling, A. *The College and University Band*, Reston, Virginia: MENC Publications, 1977

Wright, D. *The Complete Bandmaster*, Oxford: Pergamon Press, 1963

   Scoring for Brass Band (enlarged edn), London: John Baker, 1967

Wright, F. (ed.). *Brass Today*, London: Besson, 1957

The following journals also contain articles of interest:

Band International, Journal of the Military Music Society (ed. E.W.J. Bevan), vol. 2, no. 1; no. 2, 1980

British Bandsman, 'A Brief History of Wind Band Music', vol. 28, no. 500, 1911

Journal of the British Association of Symphonic Bands and Wind Ensembles (ed. K. Thompson), vol. 1, Spring 1982; Autumn 1982

Music in Education, vol. 42, June 1978

The Trumpeter, Journal of the National School Band Association (ed. V. Smith), no. 74, Summer 1980; no. 75, Winter 1980; no. 76, Summer 1981

Index